VEN
ICE

T0001525

Travel with Marco Polo
Insider Tips

INSIDER TIP
Your shortcut
to a great
experience

MARCO POLO
TOP HIGHLIGHTS

PIAZZA SAN MARCO ⭐1
Possibly the most beautiful piazza in the world – you will be amazed by its grandeur.

➤ p. 35

GIUDECCA ⭐2
The walk from the Redentore church, Andrea Palladio's masterpiece, to the luxurious Molino Stucky mill is quite magnificent.
📷 *Tip: From the shoreline you can capture the morning sun reflected in the lagoon.*

➤ p. 58

PALAZZO DUCALE ⭐3
The corridors of power: from here the doges ruled the mighty maritime republic.

➤ p. 39

BASILICA DI SAN MARCO ⭐4
Gold and glittering splendour: St Mark's Basilica is simply incredible, with a wealth of mosaics, precious stones and breathtaking interiors (photo).
📷 *Tip: Crouch down to capture better close-ups of the basilica's many details.*

➤ p. 38

CAMPANILE DI SAN MARCO ⭐5
This high point provides the most fantastic overview of the city.
📷 *Tip: There's nowhere better to photograph the swallows soaring above St Mark's Square.*

➤ p. 36

MURANO ⭐

Watch the glass-blowers create stunning works of art and then browse around one of the many artisan shops.

📷 *Tip: The glass-blowers' cheeks filled with air always make a good photo.*

➤ p. 61

CIMITERO DI SAN MICHELE ⑦

Beautiful and melancholic: a cypress-lined walk on Venice's cemetery island.

📷 *Tip: In spring, the blossom in front of the weathered gravestones provides great contrast.*

➤ p. 61

FRARI ⑧

If you are visiting just one church, then let this be the one: here, the great and the good of the art world have been immortalised, from Titian and Canova to Bellini and Donatello.

➤ p. 52

PONTE DI RIALTO ⑨

The world-famous bridge – packed with souvenir stalls but nevertheless wonderful as it stretches elegantly across the canal.

➤ p. 50

DO MORI ⑩

Savoury appetisers and a glass of wine: this is day-to-day living, Venetian style, in the city's oldest stand-up bar.

➤ p. 68

CONTENTS

Campo San Giacomo di Rialto

⏱	Plan your visit	☂	Rainy day activities
€–€€€	Price categories	🐷	Budget activities
(*)	Premium-rate phone number	👹	Family activities
		🚩	Classic experiences

(📖 A2) Refers to the removable pull-out map
(0) Located off the map

CONTENTS

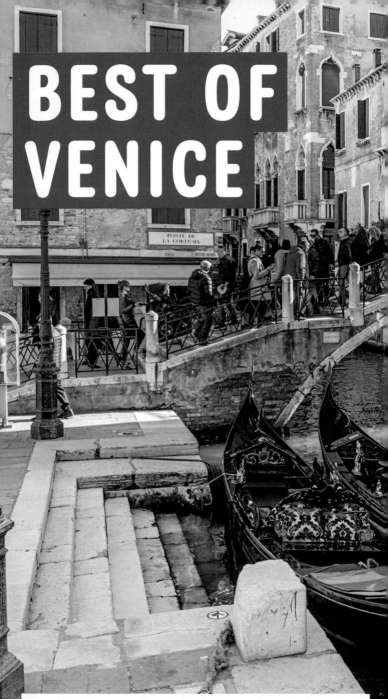

BEST OF
VENICE

The water washes against the city's foundations: a side canal at Campo Manin

BEST 🐾

WHEN IT RAINS

ACTIVITIES TO BRIGHTEN YOUR DAY

DISCOVER THE DOGE'S PALACE

Over almost 1,000 years, 120 doges determined the fate of the maritime republic from this gigantic complex of buildings. It is no wonder that the halls are so elaborately decorated (photo).
➤ p. 39, Sightseeing

MARITIME HERITAGE

The colourful collection of historic vessels at the *Padiglione delle Navi,* near the Ponte dell'Arsenale over the Rio della Tana, harks back to the glory days of the maritime republic. This exciting exhibition is also ideal for children.
➤ p. 46, Sightseeing

ART OF THE 20TH CENTURY

Modern art comes as a welcome change in a city that is so strongly associated with 500 years of painting. In the *Collezione Peggy Guggenheim* you will find works by all the great 20th-century masters.
➤ p. 57, Sightseeing

MAKE YOUR OWN MASK

Creative masks are a trademark of the Venice Carnival. At Ca' Macana, you can not only buy one of these works of art, but also spend a couple of hours learning how to make one.
➤ p. 85, Shopping

PLACE YOUR BETS!

If it rains, you can spend your days playing roulette, blackjack or poker in the elegant surroundings of composer Richard Wagner's final home; the *Casino* is located in a magnificent Renaissance palace.
➤ p. 93, Nightlife

CELEBRITY SPOTTING

With a bit of luck you will spot Hollywood stars in the flesh: simply order a cocktail in the bar of one of the well-known luxury hotels (Gritti Palace, Hotel Danieli or Hotel Bauer Palazzo, for example) and wait to see who passes by.

BEST
ON A BUDGET
FOR SMALLER WALLETS

THE CITY'S GRAVE SIDE

At *San Michele*, poets and philosophers, artists and industrialists are buried side by side. Experience pure melancholy in the celebrity cemetery free of charge. Afterwards, you can return to the land of the living!
➤ p. 61, Sightseeing

DRINK IN A DREAM LOCATION

Instead of splashing out on a pricey dinner to enjoy one of the restaurant terraces by the water, for example at the *Linea d'Ombra* (photo), simply order a spritz or other aperitif. Arrive before 6.30pm and let them know you would just like a drink.
➤ p. 72, Eating & drinking

PARTY UNDER THE STARS

In the summer, it's easy to chat with the locals while enjoying a glass of wine, as many of the squares turn into open-air party venues where there's no entry fee and you don't have to buy drinks. Some of the most popular spots are the *campi Santa Margherita* and *San Bartolomeo*.
➤ p. 94, Nightlife

EAT LIKE THE LOCALS

Small, cosy and inexpensive trattorias still exist. In most cases, the menu is short, but the dishes will all be home-cooked. A tip: at lunchtime, simply follow the bricklayers and other tradespeople because, wherever they eat, servings will be big and prices low.
p. 68, Eating & drinking

WHISK THROUGH THE LAGOON

Lagoon excursions on a hired boat are great fun, but they come at a price. Instead, take the *vaporetto line 14* where you pay public transport fees for the journey from San Zaccaria in St Mark's Square to Punta Sabbioni. In good weather you can enjoy fabulous views of the islands of Lido and Sant'Erasmo.

BEST 👧
WITH CHILDREN

GET CREATIVE IN A MUSEUM

Local museums offer numerous guided tours and workshops for children, for example the *Museo Querini Stampalia* (you'll find information on their websites).
➤ p. 43, Sightseeing

FUN AT THE LIDO

In summer, of course, children love to build sandcastles and swim in the Adriatic Sea. A trip to the *Lido* makes a great day out. There's a playground next to the planetarium at Lungomare D'Annunzio and two bicycle rentals at the *vaporetto* station.
➤ p. 59, Sightseeing

LION HUNT

The lion, symbol of Venice, can be found carved in stone all over the city: on front doors, façades and columns. Who can find the most lions? Why not go on a city safari through the lanes of the old city?

LAGOON ADVENTURE

The lagoon offers so many fascinating things for children to explore: ancient fortifications with turrets and battlements, salt marshes and reed beds – home to numerous bird species. And you can explore the lagoon's lesser-known islands either on a guided tour or by hiring a boat!
➤ p. 58, Sightseeing

FASCINATING QUESTIONS

How did the Venetians build such stunning palaces on sand and mud? How long did it take to make a gondola? If your children bombard you with these kinds of questions, take them on a guided tour especially designed for children, for example on boat building. Almost all city guides offer *topics for children*.
➤ p. 125, Good to know

BEST ⚑

CLASSIC EXPERIENCES

PROMENADE BY THE WATER

A stroll down the 1.2-km *Zattere* quay in Dorsoduro with views of the Giudecca Canal will make your heart sing. Enjoy the pure Venice feeling!
➤ p. 54, Sightseeing

TITIAN, TINTORETTO & CO.

From momentous biblical scenes by the great masters of the Renaissance to landscape paintings of the Baroque and Rococo periods: the *Galleria dell'Accademia* contains the very essence of Venetian painting.
➤ p. 55, Sightseeing

LACE ISLAND

Lacemaking used to be a highly regarded profession, and Venetian lace was said to be the best in the world. Find out all about it at the museum on the island of *Burano* (photo).
➤ p. 61, Sightseeing

LIVELY FESTIVALS

With great gusto the Venetians celebrate several smaller festivals throughout the year. These, including the *Asparagus Festival in Cavallino,* the *Fishermen's Festival of Malamocco* and the *Wine Festival on Sant'Erasmo*, are well worth attending.
➤ p. 100, Festivals & events

TRAVEL BY GONDOLA

A cliché, yes, but so enjoyable! Instead of looking down your nose at all the tourists taking pictures of each other on the gondolas, why not try it yourself? Once you have glided along the silent canals, you'll understand the magic.
➤ p. 125, Good to know

CATCH OF THE DAY

Al fresco seafood: you'll find the freshest fish and *frutti di mare* along the shore of the Canal Grande in San Polo, on the stalls of the fish market and the Mercato di Rialto.

GET TO KNOW VENICE

It's not just gondolas and cruise ships – even the vegetables arrive by boat

DISCOVER VENICE

As well as its famous Carnival, Venice celebrates the summer Festa del Redentore

A glass of wine with a view of the Canal Grande, the gentle sound of water lapping the shore, black gondolas gliding past pompous palaces: it's almost too much to absorb in one go. Venice has thousands of hidden corners and secret alleys, and whenever you think you've finally got to grips with the city, the picture slips away from you again ... But stay calm. After all, you don't have to understand Venice from day one.

THE LIVING PAST

And the more often you come, the more pictures you will see. There's picture-postcard Venice, whose stone bridges and palaces are frozen in time. And there's Disneyland Venice, full of kitsch and cheap souvenir tat. And then there's the dream image that rises out of the murky water of the Canal Grande as you float by in a gondola, enraptured by the amazing façades of the waterside pala-

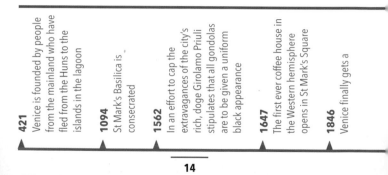

421
Venice is founded by people from the mainland who have fled from the Huns to the islands in the lagoon

1094
St Mark's Basilica is consecrated

1562
In an effort to cap the extravagances of the city's rich, doge Girolamo Priuli stipulates that all gondolas are to be given a uniform black appearance

1647
The first ever coffee house in the Western hemisphere opens in St Mark's Square

1846
Venice finally gets a

zzi: they're fabulous and yet morbid, full of precious frescoes and crumbling plaster; testimonies to bygone power. In your mind's eye you'll see the doge with his army of servants, the rustling gowns of the overdressed Rococo ladies, and Giacomo Casanova himself lounging on a terrace.

THE REALITY OF EVERYDAY LIFE

In contrast, there's everyday life in the form of a cursing delivery man moving blenders and microwaves from a freight barge to balance on his handcart and deliver to one of the few shops selling household goods. You'll see children laughing in a school playground, dogs strolling along the Lido beach, and old ladies shopping at the market near the Rialto bridge. Make the effort to get up at 6.30am just to see how busy it already is on the Canal Grande! Life here is never boring. Just relax and watch the comings and goings, wander through the maze of alleys and lanes – there's always something new to discover. And it's not all art and museums! Of course, Venice has plenty of those, but by the same token it's not an open-air museum, but a living, lively city where people work and relax, love and argue.

> **INSIDER TIP**
> **Rush hour on the Canal Grande**

FEWER & FEWER SHOPS ...

It's easy to forget how tiring everyday life is, how many inconveniences the people who live here have to endure. Being jostled every morning and evening, on the way to and from work, by the vast numbers of day-trippers on *vaporetti*, or

permanent connection to the mainland: a railway bridge to Mestre; at 3.2km it was once the longest in the world

2003 Work begins on the MOSE flood defences

2014 Mayor Giorgio Orsoni and 34 politicians and building contractors are arrested on charges of money laundering, embezzlement and extortion in connection with the MOSE project

2019 After years of debate, entry fees for day-trippers come into effect. Venice experiences its worst flooding since 1966 with water levels rising to 187cm above sea level

battling their way with a pram up and down bridges through the throng of visitors to the only remaining baker in the district. It's not all *la dolce vita*. Bakers are becoming increasingly few and far between, as are butchers and other independent shops that stock the everyday basics. There's more money to be earnt with souvenirs than with yoghurt and tinned tomatoes, which is why the number of "ordinary" shops has more than halved over the past 30 years.

... FOR A DWINDLING POPULATION OF TRUE VENETIANS

Today's Venetians do the weekly family shop in the vast supermarkets on the mainland. If indeed they have a family: the population of Venice is ageing and children are scarce. Italy has one of the lowest birth rates in the world, and more so in Venice than anywhere else. The demographic pyramid has been turned upside down, and today there are almost five times as many 60-year-old Venetians than there are under-20s. Why? The costs for food and consumer goods of all kinds are higher in Venice than elsewhere, everyday life is more difficult and local taxes are hefty. But the main reasons young families are leaving is because property prices have soared as the result of mass tourism. Wealthy foreigners will buy an apartment in Venice regardless of what it costs, leaving locals with no chance of affordable living.

In the 1950s, the population of Venice was 175,000; today there are only 55,000, and every year a few hundred more leave the city. They usually only move a few kilometres away to *terra firma*, where everything is easier and more modern. For centuries, this fertile land was the domain of the Venetian Maritime Republic; its greatest expansion to the mainland was in the middle of the 15th century, when it assimilated towns and cities such as Treviso, Padua, Vicenza and Verona. But then the Ottomans conquered Constantinople and from the 16th century were engaged in a bitter war with the Venetians for the Mediterranean trade centres. It was the beginning of the end of the powerful Serenissima.

STUDENT FLAIR

Today, Venice is also a centre for science and research. And, of course, it has a university. Students from all over the world are drawn here, in particular for its architecture faculty. As a result, a creative and lively local scene has developed in the quarters of Dorsoduro and Cannaregio in particular that hardly any visitors know about. Thanks to the university, there are also a number of student pubs charging sensible prices, as well as lounges and clubs for chilling and letting your hair down – to say nothing of the venerable cafés, original trattorie and exclusive restaurants charging eye-watering prices.

BUILT IN A SWAMP

This city on water is a miracle of humanity. Who on earth had the crazy idea of building a town in the middle of a swamp? Venice was born out of need; its

Caffè Florian in St Mark's Square – the city's oldest, most famous and perhaps most expensive café

founding was an act of desperation: where else could the people go to escape persecution by the Huns and Lombards who, from the year AD 500, descended on the fertile mainland like locusts, stealing and pillaging? The people fled to the marshes, to the malaria-infested no-man's-land that, over the centuries, became a 7.5-km² artificially created urban area. It took millions of wooden posts and over 400 bridges.

SIX QUARTERS

Since the Middle Ages, Venice has been divided into six districts, the *sestieri*. The best known of them is San Marco, with the wonderful St Mark's Square at its centre. The least touristy ones are Castello, the former working-class district, and Santa Croce. San Polo is the smallest one geographically, but has the second-biggest square, Campo San Polo. The two islands of Giudecca and San Giorgio Maggiore are considered part of Dorsoduro and San Marco respectively. Cannaregio is home to the former Jewish ghetto. Decreed by the Venetian doge as the first in the world 500 years ago, sadly it soon found many imitators.

Venice generally set a number of standards, both good and bad. As a free maritime republic, the city traded with areas that were, at that time, unimaginably distant, and it was indeed a cultural melting-pot. The upper classes were accordingly well-educated and cosmopolitan. And rich. Unbelievably rich! Spices, coffee and cocoa came to Europe via Venice. So it follows that the very first coffee house of the western hemisphere also opened in Venice. That was in 1647, under the arcades of St Mark's Square.

GOLDEN ERA & PRESENT STAGNATION

Since then, the Venetians have been masters of the *arrangiarsi*, the art of getting along. They've got trade in their blood and a keen sense for commerce. That was already so in 1204 when, under the leadership of the completely blind doge Enrico Dandolo, they unceremoniously diverted the fourth crusade to Constantinople and plundered the treasures of their fellow Christians. And it applied even more so over the following centuries, when the doges brutally represented the Republic's interests both internally and externally, and Venice, the most important trading power in the eastern Mediterranean, was raking in the money. Skilled communicators, but also pretty brazen and full of themselves, the Venetians treated their competing Italian neighbours with contempt and arrogance. The Duchy of Milan, in particular, was a tedious antagonist that Venice squabbled with for centuries.

However, the tide has turned in recent decades. Formally, Venice is still the capital of the Veneto region, but Veneto's heart now beats in the boom towns on the mainland. International groups were born here, such as the clothing giants Benetton, Diesel and Stefanel, and the energy company ENI in the Venetian suburb of Marghera. There have long been plans to turn this conurbation with some 2.5 million inhabitants and a workforce of more than one million people into a dynamic metropolis, creating a major harbour at Chioggia that would serve the entire Mediterranean. But, as is so often the case in Italy, there was a lot of talking, discussion and arguing – and then everything was put on hold.

FLOODING & MASS TOURISM

There is another, rather shameful story involving MOSE (Modulo Sperimentale Elettromeccanico), the proposed flood protection project. This once-in-a-century undertaking turned into a licence to print money for corrupt managers and politicians. Over a million euros have been misappropriated so far, and the head of the Venetian water authority ended up in jail along with the then mayor. The men were more interested in their bank accounts than the lagoon. The Venetians call it *una vergogna*, a disgrace; they never really warmed to the idea of this vast flood protection system. Many of them don't believe you should interfere with nature in such a radical way and feel that wellies are a much easier solution.

Around 30 million tourists visit Venice every year, and that number is constantly increasing. It's not doing the lagoon's fragile ecosystem any good – but how can this problem be solved? Limit the number of tourists allowed in? Charge an entry fee? The Venetians will give you so many different opinions that you'll be utterly confused. But one thing is certain: far from dead, Venice is very much alive. So don't wait any longer, and just throw yourself into its fabulous chaos!

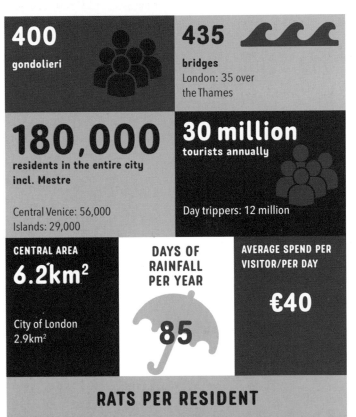

AT A GLANCE

400
gondolieri

435
bridges
London: 35 over
the Thames

180,000
residents in the entire city
incl. Mestre

Central Venice: 56,000
Islands: 29,000

30 million
tourists annually

Day trippers: 12 million

CENTRAL AREA
6.2 km²

City of London
2.9 km²

**DAYS OF
RAINFALL
PER YEAR**

85

**AVERAGE SPEND PER
VISITOR/PER DAY**

€40

RATS PER RESIDENT

More than one, that's for sure ...

CARNIVAL

Annual Carnival days: 14

ONE QUARTER

Proportion of residential
accommodation that is
rented out to tourists

UNDERSTAND VENICE

THE DARK SIDE OF THE FORCE

Were doges really to be envied? On accepting the position, a doge took on the highest office of the most powerful city state on Earth. But then he was not allowed to leave the Republic without permission, nor was he permitted to choose his own advisors or receive emissaries in private. Accepting gifts was also forbidden, as was going to a café or theatre, let alone abdicating of his own accord. He was not even allowed to write letters to his wife without it passing through the censor's hands. In fact, after the 11th century, the doges didn't have any real power at all. Starting in CE 697, they reigned high-handedly and autonomously as medieval sovereigns. They negotiated with emperors and popes, decided on war or peace independently and even named their own successor. However, in 1032, one particular doge fell victim to his own lust for power and attempted to turn the office of doge into a hereditary title. In a flash, both he and his son were assassinated and the authority of his successors radically restricted. Degraded to simple executive officers, they were placed under the surveillance of the infamous Council of the Ten, a kind of medieval state security service. In later years this meant that few suitable people were prepared to accept what had once been such a prestigious office.

DO YOU SPEAK VENEXIANO?

Between themselves, the Venetians speak the dialect they have used for time immemorial. In some aspects, it is similar to Spanish, but it follows its own rules, not only in terms of pronunciation but also in spelling and grammar. The people who live on the lagoon love to contract long (place) names. For example, San Zanipolo is an abbreviated form of the famous church of Santi Giovanni e Paolo, and San Zan Degola is San Giovanni Decollato (John the Beheaded). As for the pronunciation, many consonants are pronounced differently; a typical case is *amico* that turns into the Spanish-sounding *amigo*. In Venetian a sharp "s" often takes the place of the Italian *ch* and *sh* sounds – *cento* is pronounced *sento*. And, "z" often becomes "x". A classic example is one you will notice on advertisements for many trattorias: *cucina venexiana*.

THE MASKED BALL

The city on the lagoon turns into a fairytale land in the last one and a half weeks before Lent when tens of thousands of people wander through Venice in their imaginative robes, and the streets and squares become populated by characters from the *commedia dell'arte*. For centuries, this masquerading made it possible for Venetians to escape the watchful eye of the state for a short time at least. The occupier Napoleon, however, was suspicious and thought that conspiracy could flourish behind the masks and completely forbid the masquerade. It was not reintroduced until 1979.

Since then, hoteliers, restaurant owners and sponsors rub their hands in glee when hordes of people from all over the world, craving fun and masquerading, make their way to the city in what used to be the low season in order to pose and promenade around the city. And, if their finances allow it, they throw private parties in rented palaces. Although very few locals mingle with the masses, and the number of spectators and paparazzi probably far exceed those in disguise (and although Mickey Mouse and King Kong masks can be seen among the classical costumes), everybody agrees that being there to experience the unique atmosphere compensates for the city's drastically increased room rates.

OLD FOLKS & SPRING VEGETABLES

The fruit and vegetable market on the Rialto Bridge is in a central location right at the heart of the city's tourist area – and yet it is an authentically Venetian place. Early in the morning you'll hear scraps of dialect as Signora Maria inspects the aubergines on offer from Vincenzo and asks him when he's finally going to get the tender young artichokes from Sant'Erasmo island back in again. Yes, that's right. Most of the vegetables are actually grown in the lagoon, rather than being carted in from far away. Sant'Erasmo is Venice's kitchen garden, where people make a living from agriculture rather than tourism. This

The classic Carnival mask is the kind that covers just half your face

The small island of Poveglia as seen from the southern end of the Lido at Malamocco

means they tend vegetable beds rather than hotel beds. The question is how much longer will they be able to do this. The islanders are becoming fewer and getting older. Vincenzo is in his early sixties and is considered a spring chicken. His sons moved to the mainland years ago. Who will still be around in 20 years' time to grow the typical purple artichokes is anyone's guess. So perhaps you'd better head to Sant'Erasmo island sooner rather than later.

BLACK, SLENDER & CHIC

They are a little over 10m long and almost 1.5m wide, weigh 350kg empty, and consist of a total of 280 individual elements including the walnut oarlock *(forcola)* and the seven-pronged iron prow *(ferro)* which weighs 20kg. It is estimated that around 10,000 gondolas were in operation on Venice's canals in the 16th century. Today, only about 400 *gondolieri* are still active. However, there is no sign of an end coming to the gondola business. Thanks to the trade being passed on within families, there is no difficulty in finding recruits and the money is good, in spite of five months of slow business in the off season. The order books of the *squeri* – the gondola boatyards, the most photogenic of which can be visited on Campo San Trovaso not far from the Zattere – are booked up for years to come. A newly built boat, painted in traditional black, will set the new owner back about 15,000 euros.

GENTRIFICATION ALLA VENEZIANA

The waters around Venice's *centro storico* are sprinkled with little islands, many of which have a quite special history. Poveglia's former – and future – uses are particularly interesting. This island in front of the Lido in the south of the lagoon may measure only 7 hectares, but it was once a sanctuary for deposed doges and a quarantine station when epidemics raged. In the 20th century, however, the island, along with its few desolate buildings, vineyards and fruit trees, fell into a deep sleep. It was unexpectedly awakened from its slumber in 2014 when the Italian government decided to quickly privatise a number of prime pieces of real estate to help alleviate its major budget deficit. The jewel in the crown, so to speak, was to be the island of Poveglia – the last open patch of land in the lagoon city. But a group of strong-minded Venetians decided to put a spoke in the government's plans because they did not like the idea of another island being transformed into a luxury resort by some well-heeled hotel chain. Using the rallying slogan *Poveglia per tutti* (Poveglia for all), they launched a Facebook campaign to encourage their fellow citizens to fork out 99 euros a piece to collectively buy the rights to the island for 99 years. The proclaimed goal was to "turn the island into a public park in which children can play and friends can have grill parties". After the decisive Internet auction, the responsible authorities did in fact decline the highest lease

TRUE OR FALSE?

CARNIVAL MAD

It is true that the Venetians love their Carnival. Despite the vast numbers of tourists parading across St Mark's Square in sophisticated costumes, very few residents will want to miss the spectacle. Every self-respecting Venetian has a new costume made every year – and they don't come cheap. The standard equipment for joining the crowds in disguise comprises a mask and a black cloak, and these can be found in all the city's traditional households.

A DOOMED CITY?

Venice is being reclaimed by the sea. Scientists have been warning for many years that rising sea levels will lead to increased periods of flooding. Dredging of the oil tanker and cruise ship lanes has resulted in ever-faster currents entering the lagoon. Although the MOSE flood defences have been under construction for a long time, they are not yet operational. Also, the dreaded *moto ondoso*, the wake of the motorboats, is a slow but constant threat to the foundations of the old buildings which rest on wooden posts. Venice is gradually crumbling and sinking, a millimetre at a time. But a speed limit on the canals is not an option!

offer from a real estate speculator – half a million euros – as insufficient. Thus, for the time being, the island remains in the hands of the state, and who knows, maybe it really will be opened to the public.

ACQUA ALTA

Venice is up to its neck in water. The waters of the Adriatic regularly flood St Mark's Square and large areas of the centre. Wading through knee-high water in wellies is something tourists find rather amusing, but for the Venetians it's a constantly recurring nightmare. The problem has existed for as long as Venice has, and it has got worse in the past 50 years. There are many reasons for this, but some of them are manmade: man has interfered with the delicate ecosystem by digging out access channels for oil tankers on the way to Marghera, and has cheerfully pumped out groundwater to fill the needs of industry on the mainland. So what to do? The mammoth MOSE (Modulo Sperimentale Elettromeccanico) project began in 2003. It comprises 78 steel barriers that are to be rooted at the three entrances to the lagoon and lift up automatically to seal off Venice when there is a risk of flooding. Environmental organisations are sceptical. The floods of the Adriatic wash harmful substances out of the lagoon; without this exchange of water, the lagoon would be destroyed by its own dirt.

Lauded by Italian politicians as a masterpiece of Italian engineering skills, MOSE itself is now at risk of going under: in a swamp of corruption.

More than 30 contractors, administration managers and politicians, including Giorgio Orsoni, the former mayor of Venice, have been arrested for misappropriating funds. A healthy proportion of the 5.5 million euros that the lock system is to cost has been fed into foreign countries through accounts in San Marino. The Venetians are appalled and will continue to reach for their wellies when necessary. You'll find a few impressive photos of "Venice flooded" e.g. at *short.travel/ven12* and *short.travel/ven11*.

THE FIRST GLOBETROTTER

Of course, he deserves special mention in a guidebook that is named after him: Marco Polo, who was born

Acqua alta (high water): exciting for visitors, but a serious problem for residents

in Venice in 1254 and died there 70 years later, is still considered the quintessential globetrotter, driven by a thirst for knowledge and a yearning to see distant places. The merchant's son was only an adolescent when he set out across the Adriatic on his way to Asia; he spent many years in China and only returned by sea to the lagoon 24 years later. In Genoese custody as a prisoner of war, he dictated his travel report *Il Milione* to a fellow prisoner; it became a bestseller in the Middle Ages and played a decisive role in shaping the Europeans' geographical notion of Asia. The Polo family's house was located not far from the Rialto Bridge where the Teatro Malibran stands today.

A LION NAMED MARK

No, the Venetians were not the only people to take the lion as their heraldic animal. But nobody else gave the king of the beasts two wings and placed a book between its front paws. There are different explanations of why this strange hybrid creature should represent Saint Mark of all people. Today, the number of representations of the stone big cat is bewildering. You will see the Lion of Saint Mark on façades, cornices and capitals, on chimneys, graves, flowerpots, paintings, and there are statues of him all over the city.

SIGHT SEEING

Venice's abundance of churches, art, artefacts and unique architecture is largely thanks to the doges, who were keen to show off their power and wealth by collecting paintings and other treasures from all corners of their maritime empire. Naturally, they only ever commissioned the very best architects, painters and artisans.

Dive straight into the thick of things with a ride on a *vaporetto* down the Canal Grande; there's no lovelier way to start your Venetian adventure, beginning at the railway station or the Piazzale Roma and continuing past the fabulous façades of palaces and churches. It

Whether you choose a gondola or a *vaporetto*: a cruise on the Canal Grande is a must

gives you a good idea of Venetian daily life because the Canal Grande is the Venetians' main thoroughfare.

Venice is divided into six districts, the *sestieri*, each with its own individual character, although one thing applies to them all: it is not always possible to plan your route exactly. The lanes of Venice are a maze of stone, and you often discover the best bits when you have got lost once again. If you really don't know where you are, keep looking for one of the yellow signs pointing to "Rialto", "San Marco" or the "Ferrovia" (railway station).

THE SESTIERI – AN OVERVIEW

CANAL GRANDE p. 30
Explore Venice's most beautiful "street" by boat

SAN POLO & SANTA CROCE p. 50
The best markets and biggest squares – alive day and night

DORSODURO p. 53
Contemporary art and creativity – the cultural heart of Venice

Via della Libertà

Fondamenta de Cannaregio

Strada Nova

Venezia Santa Lucia

Canal Grande

Calle Dietro Ai Magazzini

📍 Frari ★

Galleria dell'Accademia ★ 📍

San Basilio Pier

Fondamente Zattere

Canale della Giudecca

Fondamente San Biagio

Sacca San Biagio

Giudecca ★

500 m
547 yd

MARCO POLO HIGHLIGHTS

★ **PIAZZA SAN MARCO**
The heart of Venice with elegant shops and cafés ➤ p. 35

★ **BASILICA DI SAN MARCO**
Gold and silver splendour in St Mark's Cathedral ➤ p. 38

★ **CAMPANILE DI SAN MARCO**
The best overview of the city ➤ p. 36

★ **PALAZZO DUCALE**
The beating heart of La Serenissima for a thousand years ➤ p. 39

★ **PONTE DI RIALTO**
The symbol of a former economic power ➤ p. 50

⭐ Murano
⭐ Cimitero di San Michele
⭐ Ponte di Rialto
⭐ Piazza San Marco
⭐ Basilica di San Marco
⭐ Palazzo Ducale
⭐ Campanile di San Marco

da Nova
Bacino di San Marco
Isola di San Giorgio Maggiore
Via Giuseppe Garibaldi
Riva dei Sette Martiri
Secco Marina
Viale IV Novembre
Viale Piave
Viale Vittorio Veneto
Fondamenta Manin

The fact that the opening days and times of the museums vary greatly and change frequently is rather impractical.

What's more, there are no set conditions for reduced admission fees. In any case, it is always a good idea to ask if you can enter and to have your passport or other means of identification with you. Entrance fees for museums start at 5 euros (Museo del Merletto on Burano, Casa Goldoni) and can go up to 10 or 12 euros (Scuola Grande di San Rocco and Accademia respectively). The *I Musei di Piazza San Marco* pass costs 20 euros and allows you to visit all four museums on Piazza San Marco. The *Museum Pass*, 24 euros, includes all of the city's museums except the clock tower and the Palazzo Fortuny – available online at *veneziaunica.it*.

For 45 euros, the *MUVE Friend Card Blu (visitmuve.it)* offers free admission to the museums in St Mark's Square as well as almost all city museums. The *MUVE Friend Card Rosso* is valid for people under the age of 27, costs 25 euros and offers the same conditions. EU citizens under the age of 18 have free admission to the three state museums – Accademia, Galleria Franchetti and Museo d'Arte Orientale – while 18 to 25 year-olds are granted a reduction.

The Tourism Association's website *veneziaunica.it* gives the best overview on the Internet (also in English and easy to navigate). All city museums are included under *visitmuve.it* (also in English). Fifteen of the most important churches in art history have joined forces to form the *Associazione Chiese di Venezia/Chorus* (chorusvenezia.org). The Chorus Pass, a joint ticket for 12 euros (8 euros for students under 29, families 24 euros) allows you to visit these places of worship and is valid for an unlimited period. Individual admission to the important churches costs around 3 euros each.

WHERE TO START?

Once you arrive in Venice, head straight for the **Piazza San Marco** (*J–K 7–8*) – preferably on board one of the Line 1 or 2 *vaporetti* that travel along the Canal Grande from the railway station, coach and car parks on Piazzale Roma. The 4.1/4.2 and 5.1/5.2 lines are also a good way to become acquainted with Venice as they travel around the entire historical centre. The best bird's eye panoramas are from the viewing galleries in the Campanile of San Marco or San Giorgio Maggiore.

CANAL GRANDE

This is Venice's main thoroughfare, frequented by barges, water taxis, buses and speedboats. It leads from the railway station or Piazzale Roma to the Dogana da Mar, the old customs office, crowned by a golden globe (journey time between 20 and 50 minutes).

The elegantly curved Ponte della Costituzione, designed by Santiago Calatrava

En route you pass the magnificent façades of palaces and churches in sensationally close succession, an array of grandeur almost unrivalled on earth.

1 PONTE DELLA COSTITUZIONE

It's a real bone of contention, this modern bridge with glass parapets and a herringbone design. Some people think it's hideous beyond words; others think it's great. Its creator and the municipality have even battled it out in court. What is undeniable is that this 94m-long pedestrian bridge, which was designed by Santiago Calatrava and has spanned the Canal Grande between Piazzale Roma and the station since 2008, is something completely different. *Stop: Piazzale Roma, Ferrovia | ᗐ C–D5*

2 FONDACO DEI TURCHI

The complex of buildings was erected in the 13th century. Four hundred years later, Turkish merchants lived and carried out their business here leading to the name that is commonly used today. A rather insane total redevelopment in the 19th century robbed it of its Venetian-Byzantine character. Only the characteristic towers on the sides and the wide columned hall in between have been preserved. Today, the prominent building is the site of the 🐾 *Museum of Natural History (Museo di Storia Naturale | June–Oct Tue–Sun 10am–6pm, Nov–May Tue–Fri 9am–5pm, Sat/Sun 10am–6pm | msn. visitmuve.it)* – great for families! The highlights include the aquarium and a dinosaur hall with a complete skeleton found in the South Sahara. *Stop: San Stae | ᗐ G4*

If you want to see how the aristocrats lived in the 18th century, visit the Ca' Rezzonico

🖪 PALAZZO VENDRAMIN CALERGI

This imposing Renaissance palace built by Mauro Codussi and the Lombardo brothers around 1500 is firmly located in history as the place where German composer Richard Wagner spent the last part of his life. Today, it is a gamblers' mecca: the city's casino *(casinovenezia.it)* with its night club are located behind the windows with their round arches. *Stop: San Marcuola | ⟐ G4*

🖪 SAN STAE

The main attraction of this 17th-century church is the beautiful Palladian-style façade added by the Swiss architect Domenico Rossi in 1709. Inside, there are several remarkable paintings from the early 18th century, including works by Giambattista Tiepolo, Giovanni Battista Piazzetta and Sebastiano Ricci. *Campo San Stae 3013 | Mon–Sat 2–5pm | stop: San Stae | ⟐ G4*

🖪 CA' PESARO

Even if you were not especially interested in the collections of oriental and modern art that are housed in Ca' Pesaro, you would still marvel at this massive Baroque complex with its marble façade that dominates the southern side of the Canal Grande. It is Baldassare Longhena's masterpiece and its construction took almost 60 years to complete. The splendid collection in the *Galleria d'Arte Moderna* includes works by Max Klinger, Gustav Klimt, Wassily Kandinsky, Max Klee, Auguste Rodin, Marc Chagall and Giorgio De Chirico.

Admirers of art from East and Southeast Asia will find what they are looking for in the *Museo d'Arte Orientale* on the top floor with its collection of armour, textiles and artworks from China, Japan and Indonesia, as well as an important exhibition of Japanese paintings from the Edo period from the early 17th to mid-19th centuries. *Tue–Sun 10am–5pm, April–Oct until 6pm | capesaro. visitmuve.it | stop: San Stae |* ⏱ *1½ hrs |* ⌖ *H4*

6 CA' D'ORO/GALLERIA GIORGIO FRANCHETTI

INSIDER TIP
Architectural jewel in a top spot

Nowhere else along the Canal Grande can you find a façade that is more delicate and precious than this one.

The "Golden House" is the master-work of the Venetian late-Gothic period at the transition to the Renaissance. Its painstakingly restored exterior, which was originally decorated with gold leaf and coloured marble, looks like Burano lace carved in stone. *Baron Franchetti's art collection* is exhibited inside. It includes several masterpieces such as Andrea Mantegna's *St Sebastian*, Titian's *Venus*, Vittore Carpaccio's *Annunciation and Death of the Blessed Virgin*, as well as paintings by Giovanni Bellini, Giorgione, Anthony van Dyck and many other artists. There is also an admirable collection of Flemish tapestries and Gothic and Renaissance furniture. *Tue–Sun 8.15am–7.15pm, Mon 8.15am–2pm | cadoro.org | stop: Ca' d'Oro |* ⏱ *1½ hrs |* ⌖ *H4–5*

7 PESCHERIA

The neo-Gothic building with its arcades was only constructed in 1907. However, a fish market has existed at this location since the 14th century and the neighbouring fruit and vege-table market ever since CE 1100. *Stop: Rialto or Ca' d'Oro and cross with the traghetto (gondola ferry) |* ⌖ *H5*

8 CA' FOSCARI

When you get to the *volta*, the last bend in the Canal Grande, look out for the entirely symmetrical façade of this late-Gothic palace. It was restored in 2008 by students of the university, which has its headquarters here. The palazzo used to belong to the family of the doge Francesco Foscari. In the 19th century it was used as a hospital, and later as a military barracks by the Austrian occupying forces. After that it became rather run-down, but thanks to the students and their hard graft it is once again a shining light on the Canal Grande. *Stop: Ca' Rezzonico, San Tomà |* ⌖ *F7*

9 PALAZZO GRASSI

That's a fabulous building, sliding by on the other side of the water. The changing exhibitions have been the subject of much talk for several years now. Its French patron François Pinault spares no expense when it comes to making Venice a hotspot of contem-porary art. *Wed–Mon 10am–7pm | combined ticket with Punta della Dogana | palazzograssi.it | stop: San Samuele |* ⏱ *1½ hrs |* ⌖ *F8*

10 CA' REZZONICO/MUSEO DEL SETTECENTO VENEZIANO

Even by Venetian standards, this massive palace built by Baldassare

Loghena and Giorgio Massari is a special Renaissance jewel in the Venetian crown. For part of the 18th century, it was owned by Carlo Rezzonico who later became Pope Clemens XIII. Today, the building is home to the *Museo del Settecento Veneziano* and impressively documents the opulent lifestyle of the aristocracy in the late period of the Republic. This "Museum of the 18th Century" is spread over the three floors of the palazzo. Meticulously renovated, the priceless furniture and decorations, paintings and ceiling frescoes on display provide an authentic impression of how the wealthy noble families lived during that high point in Venice's history. The carved furnishings, ceiling frescos and cabinet paintings with scenes of everyday life in Venice by Pietro Longhi are particularly outstanding. *Entrance: Fondamenta Rezzonico | Wed–Mon 10am–5pm, April–Oct 10am–6pm | carezzonico.visitmuve.it | stop: Ca' Rezzonico |* ⏱ *1½ hrs |* 🗺 *F8*

⓫ SANTA MARIA DELLA SALUTE

This epitome of a Venetian Baroque church rises up in all its glory over the south-eastern end of the Canal Grande. A fantastic building, cloaked in white marble was designed by Baldassare Longhena on an octagonal layout. The church was erected in gratitude for an end to a plague epidemic and is crowned by a mighty dome that can be seen shining from far away. The vestry is decorated with altar paintings by Titian, Tintoretto and other masters. *Daily 9am–noon and 3–5.30pm; vestry Mon–Sat 10am–noon and 3–5pm, Sun 3–5pm | stop: Salute |* ⏱ *30 mins |* 🗺 *H9*

⓬ PUNTA DELLA DOGANA

The billionaire and patron of the arts François Pinault displays a representative overview of his unique collection here – including masterpieces by stars such as Jeff Koons, Richard Serra and Damien Hirst. The building that used to be the customs house at the eastern tip of Dorsoduro is crowned with two Atlas figures holding a gilded globe. *Wed–Mon 10am–7pm | combined ticket with Palazzo Grassi | palazzograssi.it | stop: Salute |* 🗺 *J9*

SAN MARCO

This district used to be the centre of power for the maritime republic. If you lived here, you were quite clearly a member of the upper class. To this day, the names on the bells of these elegant private homes read like a Who's Who of the global (moneyed) aristocracy. It's where the city's heart beats – and it's crammed with tourists.

But no matter how many backpacks bash into you, how many selfie sticks nearly have your eye out, the Piazza San Marco is incomparable; without it, you haven't seen Venice. So get into the Doge's Palace and Saint Mark's Basilica, and up the Campanile! Then immerse yourself in the swirling masses in the alleys around the square, where an espresso at one of the tiny standing-only bars will cost a

The Punta della Dogana with its golden globe marks the southern end of the Canal Grande

fraction of what you'd be charged at one of the famous coffee houses with their lace tablecloths and orchestras on the actual square.

🔞 PIAZZA SAN MARCO ★

Napoleon's exclamation that this is "the most beautiful salon on earth" is still valid more than 200 years later. The 175-m-long, slightly trapezoid-shaped St Mark's Square, laid out more than 800 years ago, is unique and conjures up a different atmosphere depending on the season and the time of day. It has been the site of countless religious processions and a great number of very earthly festivities. The piazza has remained a stage for the vanity of both locals and tourists to this very day. And, during those

rare hours on foggy winter days or late at night when the usual masses have deserted it and it finally comes to rest, isolated dreamers will find the setting magical. However, irrespective of the time of day or the weather, once in a lifetime you must stroll across this square and under the arcades with their luxury shops. *Stop: San Marco | ⌘ J–K 7–8*

🔟 MUSEO CORRER

This city museum with its incredibly rich collections is slightly hidden behind the south-west façade of the Piazza San Marco. Here, art lovers are invited to take a journey to the roots of Venetian (art) history. The neo-Classicist rooms on the first floor display some early works by the renowned

The eye-catching Campanile di San Marco

Kingdom of Italy in the 1860s. A new attraction at the museum after ten years of restoration work are the re-opened *imperial chambers*, in which the Empress Sisi, the wife of the Hapsburg Emperor Franz Joseph, resided for a total of eight months during two trips to the city.

A large section of the second floor is reserved for the picture gallery: precious paintings and sculptures from the Veneto-Byzantine and early-Gothic periods, into the Cinquecento, the golden 16th century. Highlights include works by Jacopo Bellini and his family, as well as Lorenzo Lotto who was active one generation later and the snow-white marble statues created by Antonio Canova. However, the most famous exhibit in the museum by far is Vittorio Carpaccio's picture of two *Venetian Ladies*, painted around 1510, that supposedly shows two smug courtesans with their dogs and birds. *Summer daily 10am–7pm, winter 10am–5pm | combined ticket with Palazzo Ducale, Biblioteca Marciana and Museo Archeologico | correr.visitmuve.it | stop: Vallaresso | ⏱ 2 hrs | ⊞ J8*

sculptor Antonio Canova and there's a comprehensive overview of the major historical themes of the city on the lagoon, from seafaring, politics, administration and war history to the arts, trade and festivities. Official robes and magnificent vestments worn by dignitaries are on display along with coins and the marble Lions of Saint Mark. There are also old maritime and land maps as well as the first detailed plan of the city created by Jacopo de' Barbari around 1500. One additional focus of attention is the documentation of Venetian history from the end of the Republic in 1797 to the unification of the city with the

15 CAMPANILE DI SAN MARCO ★

It's an easy ride up this famous tower in a lift, from which eight daredevils announced in 1997 that Venice was splitting from the rest of Italy – an act of folly that earned them tremendous applause and a lawsuit. Fabulous views of the rooftops of Venice are guaranteed. The panorama not only provides you with a first, extremely helpful orientation aid but also a feeling for the unique location and structure of the city on the lagoon. This symbol of the city was originally erected in the 10th century and considerably increased in height in the 12th. The almost 100-m-high tower collapsed in 1902 but was reconstructed using the original material as much as possible. While

INSIDER TIP
Look around you!

queuing to buy tickets, you will have the opportunity to admire the marvellous Loggetta, built by Jacopo Sansovino around 1540. Venice's nobility liked to gather for a chat under its arcades that form an architectural counterpart to the Scala dei Giganti (Giants' Staircase) in the Doge's Palace opposite. *Easter–June and Oct daily 9am–7pm, July–Sept 9am–9pm,*

Nov–Easter 9.30am–3.45pm | stop: San Marco | ⏱ *30 mins |* 📖 *K8*

🔟 TORRE DELL'OROLOGIO (CLOCK TOWER)

With its blue and white façade, crowned with a Lion of Saint Mark and the large dial, the clock tower designed by Mauro Codussi sometime around 1500 marks the spot where the Mercerie enters the Piazza di San Marco. From the roof terrace, two bronze giants deafeningly strike the hour. You need to book in advance if you would like to go up *(tel. 0 41 42 73 08 92 | torreorologio. visitmuve.it)* as part of a guided tour *(in Italian: daily 1pm and 4pm, in English Mon–Wed 10am and noon, Thu–Sun 2pm and 3pm). Piazza San Marco | stop: San Marco |* 📖 *K7*

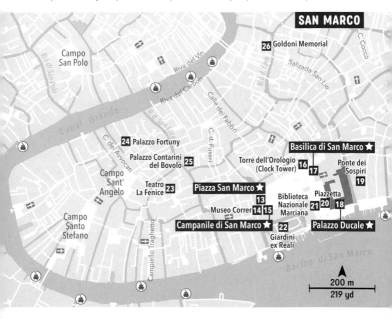

🔢 BASILICA DI SAN MARCO ⭐ 🐾

Could it be more splendid? We think not. Five domes, lavishly decorated arches and windows, mosaics, icons, the high altar with St Mark's sarcophagus and endless bronze figures. The 11th-century structure, built in the form of a Greek cross, once preserved at its heart the relics that moulded Venice's identity – the bones of Saint Mark, stolen from Alexandria in Egypt.

The main attractions: the incomparable stone mosaics that are, unfortunately, mostly covered by carpets; the sumptuously decorated, three-door iconostasis in the choir section (entrance with an extra ticket, to the right through the Capella di San Clemente); the high altar with the sarcophagus of Saint Mark; Sansovino's vestry door as well as his bronze figures; and the most precious treasure of all, the *Pala d'Oro*, a gold and enamel reredos with hundreds of precious stones created between the 10th and 14th centuries. And, of course, the magnificent *mosaics* that illustrate episodes from the Old and New Testaments and cover an area of more than 4,000m². If you want to make a closer inspection of them you should climb up to the gallery from the inner main portal.

The *Tesoro*, or treasury, stores the most valuable collection of Byzantine silver and gold in the world (here, as with the Pala d'Oro, you have to pay a small extra admission fee). Most of it came from Constantinople after the Venetians plundered the city in 1204. Although much of it was seized by Napoleon and melted down, the *Tesoro* still has an impressive collection of liturgical objects, reliquaries and carvings. You absolutely must see the *Quadriga* at close range – four world-famous bronze horses that were probably cast in Ancient Rome.

Last but not least, there are the dazzling mosaics that were applied to the walls, arches and domes of the basilica and will certainly turn the visitor's head in more ways than one, despite having been slightly damaged during the 2018 floods. They show scenes from the Old Testament (in the vestibule) and New (in the three-nave interior). Highlights include: the depiction of the Holy Ghost as a dove with the Twelve Apostles in the dome

closest to the main entrance; the Arch of the Passion with motifs from pre-Easter events; the Ascension Dome where the Saviour floats in a circle of stars supported by angels; and Christ as the blessing Pantocrator, as the "universal ruler", in the choir dome.

The queues outside the basilica can be endless, and there is so much to see inside ... Simply jump the queue by buying a Skip-the-Line ticket online *(3 euros | available April-Oct at venetoinside.com)*. Otherwise, treat yourself to the full programme, including guided tour and access to the terrace *(21.50 euros)*. Please note

INSIDER TIP
Jump the queue!

that it is not permitted to take any kind of luggage into the church. Storage facilities are available at *Ateneo San Basso (Piazzetta dei Leoncini | daily 9.30am-5.30pm); Basilica Mon-Sat 9.30am-5pm, Sun 2-4.30pm, 2-5pm in summer; galleries daily from 9.45am-4.45pm; Pala d'Oro and Tesoro Mon-Sat 9.45am-4pm, Sun 2-4pm, until 5pm in summer | basilica sanmarco.it | stop: San Marco |* ⏱ *1½ hrs | ▢ K7*

⓲ PALAZZO DUCALE ★ ⛫

The most palatial of all palaces; the Palazzo Ducale is a centre of political and legislative power, the greatest symbol of Venetian civilisation. Over

The Doge's Palace was Venice's centre of power and grandeur for centuries

the past 1,000 years, 120 doges guided the destiny of the Maritime Republic from within its walls. In the Gothic form we see today, most of the complex was constructed in the 14th and early 15th centuries.

From the Doge's Palace straight to jail: the Bridge of Sighs is aptly named

The colossal marble façade, whose lower section is interspersed with countless delicate columns and arches, deserves our greatest admiration. Take a closer look at the wonderful sculptures of *Adam and Eve* and *Drunken Noah* on the corners of the south wing, as well as the scenes on each capital of the dozens of columns!

A tour of the interior of the Doge's Palace is completely overwhelming. You pass through the main portal, the Porta della Carta, to enter the inner courtyard that is dominated by a two-storey triumphal arch, the *Arco Foscari*, and the *Scala dei Giganti* watched over by two statues, one of Neptune and one of Mars, created by Jacopo Sansavino. The greatest Italian painters of the 16th century were involved in decorating the rooms, including Tintoretto, Titian and Paolo Veronese. Most of the gigantic pictures they painted show scenes from the history of the city, from the myths surrounding its foundation to its great military victories. However, the most lasting impression is probably achieved by the *Sala del Maggior Consiglio*, a hall measuring 54×25m where as many as 1,800 members of the Grand Council would meet to elect high state officials and the members of the Signoria. Your eyes will be drawn towards Tintoretto's painting of *Paradise* on the end wall; at 7×22m it is the largest painting on canvas in the world. The tour ends with a walk over the Bridge of Sighs to the New Prison. The guided tours on "secret paths", *Itinerari*

INSIDER TIP
Top-secret locations

Segreti, which are held in Italian, French and English, are very special. Tickets can be bought at the information desk at the palace entrance or online at least 48 hours in advance (a visit to the palace is included in the ticket price). You will be able to visit the false ceiling of the Hall of the Great Council, the offices of the Grand Chancellor, the secret archives and the notorious "lead chambers" *(piombi)* where Giacomo Casanova was once incarcerated. *Daily 8.30am–6pm, April–Oct until 7pm | combined ticket with Biblioteca Marciana, Museo*

Correr and Museo Archeologico | *palazzoducale.visitmuve.it* | *stop: San Zaccaria* | ⏱ *2 hrs* | 🚊 *K8*

🔟 PONTE DEI SOSPIRI

You will almost be able to imagine that you can hear the sighs of the prisoners who once made their way, protected from any curious onlookers, over this draughty corridor from the courtroom in the Doge's Palace to the New Prison *(Palazzo delle Prigioni)*. But, only almost, because the incessant chatter of the hordes of tourists and the clicking of the cameras shooting away at the Bridge of Sighs from the Ponte della Paglia on the quay drown out everything. *Stop: San Zaccaria* | 🚊 *K8*

🔟 PIAZZETTA

The elongated area between the Campanile and Canale di San Marco, flanked on the east by the Doge's Palace and on the west by the Biblioteca Marciana, has fulfilled many functions over the centuries. For a period, gambling took place here in the open air, market stalls were set up, as were latrines, and public executions also took place here. Now it is a meeting place for people on a stroll through the city and souvenir sellers. All of these activities are watched over by Venice's first patron saint Theodor – accompanied by his crocodile and a winged Lion of Saint Mark. *Stop: San Marco* | 🚊 *K8*

🔟 BIBLIOTECA NAZIONALE MARCIANA

Jacopo Sansovino was the Florentine architect who designed this monumental Renaissance construction. The main hall of what Palladio described as "possibly the most precious, richly decorated building to be constructed since the days of the Ancient Greeks and Romans" is adorned with paintings by Veronese and Tintoretto, with the ceiling of the anteroom bearing a work by Titian. Among the most important of the approximately 900,000 volumes and 13,000 manuscripts are Marco Polo's will and the famous map of the world drawn by the monk Fra Mauro who once lived on Venice's cemetery island. *Entrance at the Museo Correr* | *Mon–Fri 8.20am–7pm, Sat 8.20am–1.30pm* | *combined ticket with Palazzo Ducale, Museo Correr and Museo Archeologico* | *marciana.venezia.sbn.it* | *stop: Vallaresso* | ⏱ *30 mins* | 🚊 *K8*

🔟 GIARDINI EX REALI

The only oasis of green in the stony heart of the city – and a very small one at that. But it's not a bad place to sit down on a shady bench to get your breath back. *Stop: San Marco* | 🚊 *J–K8*

🔟 TEATRO LA FENICE

It's hard to believe that this classical theatre is a fake. The plush red seats, the stucco, the gold – everything looks as if it dates back to the 18th century. But sadly, this world-famous opera house burnt down in 1996 and had to be rebuilt. The decision was made to rebuild it to look exactly like the original – and so it was! Even if you don't like opera, just pop in and enjoy the atmosphere! *Campo San Fantin 1965* | *daily 9.30am–6pm* | *teatrolafenice.it* | *stop: Giglio* | ⏱ *30 mins* | 🚊 *H8*

☑ PALAZZO FORTUNY

The Spanish-born painter Mariano Fortuny lived in this Gothic palazzo for more than 40 years. The highly gifted artist worked as a painter, sculptor, stage designer, lighting technician and decorator. He also designed magnificent silk fabrics and hand-painted lamps. The building has been totally renovated and now documents the work and collections of this astounding character. There are interesting temporary exhibitions on the ground floor. *Calle Pesaro 3958 | Wed–Mon 10am–6pm | fortuny.visitmuve.it | stop: Sant'Angelo | ○ 1 hr | ⅏ H7*

☑ PALAZZO CONTARINI DEL BOVOLO

If you follow a small yellow sign on the south side of Campo Marin and go round two or three corners, you will find yourself in front of this example of playful Renaissance architecture. The "Snail Shell", a spiral staircase with elegant arcades and erected around 1500, winds its way up the façade of the noble Contarini family's Gothic palace. Following its restoration, you can now climb Venice's most spectacular spiral staircase. *Daily 10am–6pm | gioiellinascostidivenezia. it | stop: Rialto, Sant'Angelo | ○ 45 mins | ⅏ H7*

INSIDER TIP
You'll need a head for heights

☑ GOLDONI MEMORIAL

Even cast in bronze, Carlo Goldoni, Venice's great comedy playwright, seems to be smiling to himself. This is not surprising seeing that the *Campo San Bartolomeo*, where the statue is located, is especially popular with

A traditional corner shop in Castello offers an insight into daily life

Venetians as a place to come and gossip or share a drink until late at night. *Stop: Rialto |* 🚇 *J6*

CASTELLO

The largest of the six municipal districts is the one with the most contrasts. Immediately behind the Doge's Palace and along the Riva Degli Schiavoni, there is the hustle and bustle of tourist life and a row of luxury hotels all next to each other. But a little further east, around Via Garibaldi and in the winding streets where the shipyard workers used to live, it is much more intimate.

Small workshops, stores, narrow streets with washing lines overhead and children playing: this is where Venice shows its friendly, everyday – occasionally a little run-down – side. But, there are also many artistic treasures waiting to be discovered here too – churches such as San Zaccaria and Santi Giovanni e Paolo with the doges' graves, or the *scuole* of the Dalmatians and Greeks. The largest green area in the city, the Giardini Pubblici, will give you a chance to catch a breath of fresh air. This is where the Biennale, a show of what is happening in the world of contemporary art and architecture, is held every two years

🚇 SAN ZACCARIA
The marble façade of this church only two or three minutes' walk from the

Doge's Palace is a real feast for the eyes. There are several important artworks inside, including one of Giovanni Bellini's most important paintings, the beautiful *Sacra Conversazione* (Maria with Child). The campanile was part of the former church erected in the 12th century and this makes it one of the oldest bell towers in Venice. *Mon–Sat 10am–noon and 4–6pm, Sun 4–6pm (please note that these times change frequently) | stop: San Zaccaria |* 🕐 *30 mins |* 🚇 *L7*

🔢 MUSEO QUERINI STAMPALIA 🏛️
The collection of paintings is the highlight of any tour of this splendid patrician's house. It includes works by Giovanni Bellini, Palma il Vecchio and Giambattista Tiepolo, as well as the genre scenes of everyday life in Venice by Pietro Longhi and Gabriele Bella. The paintings bring to life the day-to-day activities of the Venetian

INSIDER TIP
18th-century life in Venice

upper classes, including a morning walk, an evening reception, a rowing regatta and a funeral. The tour through a total of 20 rooms is especially fascinating because it will give you an idea of the magnificent surroundings enjoyed by the wealthy nobility of the 18th century, including Count Querini Stampilia. They would socialise beneath opulent ceiling frescos, Rococo stucco and chandeliers made of Murano glass, among magnificent mirrors, lacquer furniture and with a whopping 200,000 books on the shelves of the library. *Tue–Sun 10am-6pm | querinistampalia.org | stop: San Zaccaria |* ⏱ *1 hr |* 📖 *L7*

29 CAMPO DI SANTA MARIA FORMOSA

Theatre performances, festivals and bullfights used to be held here on one of the largest and most beautiful squares in Venice. These spectacles, however, are all things of the past. But this is still a great place to have an ice cream or cup of coffee and watch everyday life go by around the rather isolated (by Venetian standards) Santa Maria Formosa Church. *Stop: San Zaccaria |* 📖 *K–L6*

30 SANTI GIOVANNI E PAOLO

Official Venice attached great importance to the order of the Dominicans that commissioned this house of worship, as can be appreciated by the fact that no fewer than 27 doges have found their final resting places here. The graves provide a masterclass in the development of Venetian sculpture from the late Gothic to the Baroque period. Its colossal high point is at the grave of Alvise Mocenigo by the inner church portal. Just as impressive is the Baroque altar opposite the grave that was designed by Baldassare Longhena.

The overall impression of the interior of this mendicant order's church is conspicuously ascetic but is enhanced by some magnificent works of art, including paintings by Giovanni Bellini, Lorenzo Lotto and Paolo Veronese. Take a closer look at the Renaissance façade of the immediately adjacent *Scuola Grande di San Marco* with its wonderful reliefs and marble intarsia. *Mon–Sat 9am-6pm, Sun noon-6pm| stop: Ospedale |* ⏱ *1 hr |* 📖 *L5*

31 BARBARIA DE LE TOLE

This tranquil alley used to resound with the hammering of carpenters from dawn to dusk. It was home and workplace to craftsman who sold their *tole* (wood panels) to countries as far away as the Arab Peninsula. Although the trade eventually died out, the carpenters' street remained with their *botteghe*. The white Renaissance church of *Santa Maria dei Derelitti* is very pretty. Don't miss it! *Stop: Ospedale |* 📖 *L–M6*

32 SAN FRANCESCO DELLA VIGNA

A place of pilgrimage for lovers of architecture, this convent on the grounds of a former vineyard *(vigna)* is like an ancient temple. It is the work of Andrea Palladio, *the* star architect of the Renaissance. The classicist villas he designed for the Venetian nobility are world famous. Here he "pimped up" a place of worship. *Daily 8am-12.30pm and 3-6pm | stop: Celestia |* 📖 *N6*

33 CAMPO DE LE GATE

This quiet little square is magical. Just sit and be still for a moment. Perhaps you are familiar with some of the works by the poet Ugo Foscolo? There is a memorial plaque to the Italian writer, who lived here for a few years. *Stop: San Zaccaria |* 📖 *N7*

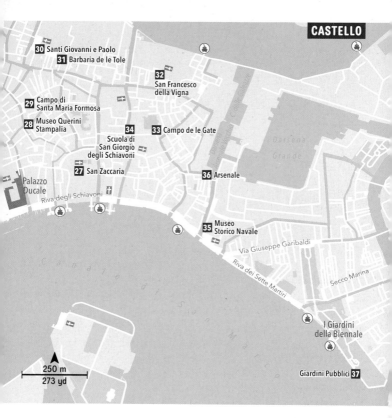

CASTELLO

30 Santi Giovanni e Paolo
31 Barbaria de le Tole
32 San Francesco della Vigna
29 Campo di Santa Maria Formosa
28 Museo Querini Stampalia
34 Scuola di San Giorgio degli Schiavoni
33 Campo de le Gate
27 San Zaccaria
Palazzo Ducale
Riva degli Schiavoni
36 Arsenale
35 Museo Storico Navale
Via Giuseppe Garibaldi
Riva dei Sette Martiri
Secco Marina
Darsena Grande
Canale di San Marco
I Giardini della Biennale
Giardini Pubblici 37

250 m
273 yd

34 SCUOLA DI SAN GIORGIO DEGLI SCHIAVONI

The brotherhood of the Slavonic people was founded in 1452 by wealthy Dalmatian merchants with the aim of supporting impoverished, old seamen from their homeland and providing education for their children. The small oratory is one of the few rooms in the city where the paintings are still surrounded by their original carved and gilded panelling. Its greatest treasure is the cycle of paintings created at the beginning of the 16th century by Vittore Carpaccio. It shows scenes from the life of the patron saints of Dalmatia – George, Trifon and Hieronymus – the history of George the "Dragon Slayer" being particularly well painted. *Mon 2.45–6pm, Tue–Sat 9.30am–1pm and 3–6pm, Sun 9.30am–1pm | stop: San Zaccaria | ⏱ 1 hr | 🗺 M7*

35 MUSEO STORICO NAVALE

The Museum of Naval History is fittingly housed in an old warehouse right next to the Arsenal and covers the history of the maritime republic from the perspective of shipping.

45

The entrance gate to the Arsenale is flanked by four lions

There are many models of battle and passenger ships, canons from five centuries, explanations of how gondolas and fortresses are built, as well as fishing nets, nautical charts, navigational equipment and pious votive pictures testifying to miraculous rescues at sea. The highlight is definitely the *Bucintoro*, the state galley from which the doge performed the annual *Marriage of the Sea* ritual. ☂ It is worth taking an extra tour of

INSIDER TIP
Explore the former maritime power

the Pavilion of Ships, a huge collection of historic vessels. You can visit the *Padiglione delle Navi (daily 11am–5pm)* at the Ponte dell'Arsenale via the Rio della Tana. *Daily 10am–5pm, April–Oct until 6pm | stop: Arsenale |* 🕐 *2 hrs |* 🗺 *N–08*

🖽 ARSENALE

This shipyard, where Venice built the ships for its gigantic navy and merchant fleet, and where weapons and gunpowder were also stored, was the centre of the largest maritime power in the Eastern Mediterranean from the 14th to the late 18th century; consequently, it was heavily guarded. In its heyday, the Arsenale employed 16,000 workers. Today, ferries and freighters are repaired in the 320,000m² area with its magnificent entrance *(Ingresso di Terra)* flanked by four lions. This is also the site of several high-tech companies, workshops and offices. Nowadays, the Italian military only presides over a small section, which is why the northern part of the arsenal recently stopped being a prohibited military area and is now open to the public. In the years when the Biennale is held, the Biennale Foundation offers free guided tours of the southern part once a week, for which you need to book a place in advance *(tel. 04 15 21 88 28 | promozione@labiennale.org)*. As the arsenals are also the headquarters of the company that is responsible for the MOSE flood protection project, you can also book guided tours of the vast lock construction here *(info@ mose-venezia.it)*. Mon–Fri, during the

Biennale daily 10am–5pm | comune. venezia.it/it/arsenaledivenezia | stop: Arsenale | N–P 6–8

🟦 GIARDINI PUBBLICI

As you might imagine, you won't see much in the way of grass or avenues of trees in Venice. So these public gardens are great for a stroll through greenery. And the *Serra*, the glasshouse of 1894, has a *caffetteria (daily 10am–8pm)* that serves sweet and savoury snacks, all organic. A very relaxed atmosphere at cocktail time. *Viale Garibaldi 1254 | serradeigiardini. org | stop: Giardini |* 🔲 *P9–10*

CANNAREGIO

The north-west district between the station and the Rialto Bridge is, on the one hand, very touristy because it's where everyone tries to push through to St Mark's Square, but on the other hand it's also the most densely populated, with only a few second homes belonging to wealthy foreigners. It includes 33 islands and lots of canals.

There are some wonderful walks along these canals and also lovely restaurants away from the city's main artery (Lista di Spagna/Rio Terà San Leonardo/Strada Nova), with terraces by the water, and bars where the locals like to come for a quick espresso. And there are numerous breathtaking palazzi on the northern shores of the Canal Grande. Be sure to visit the former Jewish Ghetto as well, which is in the middle of Cannaregio. Lovely synagogues and kosher restaurants radiate an entirely unique atmosphere

🟦 GHETTO

Located in the centre of Cannaregio, this "district within a district" was the original attempt to confine Jewish people in a specific area and served as a kind of model for all the ghettos created later throughout the world. At the beginning of the 16th century, the Senate allocated this district to be the home of the 5,000 members of the

Highlight in the Museo Storico Navale: the golden Bucintoro

The Scuola Levantina is one of four synagogues in the Ghetto

very successful and influential Jewish community. This area, whose name comes from the metal foundries (the *getti*) that were formerly located here, was conveniently surrounded by canals. Gates were added and manned by (Christian) guards, and blocks of flats were built that were rented to Jews at exorbitant rates. The names of the three sections are misleading; the "new" Ghetto Nuovo, founded in 1516, is actually 25 years older than the "old" Ghetto Vecchio. The "newest" Ghetto Novissimo was created when the area was extended around 1630.

The four magnificent synagogues in the Ghetto are well worth visiting: the *Scuola La Tedesca* built in 1528 by German Ashkenazi Jews; the four years younger *Scuola Canton* that is now in the Rococo style; the *Scuola Levantina* from the second half of the 17th century with its splendidly carved pulpit by Andrea Brustolon; and the largest *Scuola Spagnola* that is

especially impressive on account of the use of multi-coloured marble.The very informative guided tours also include a visit to the *Museo Ebraico (Sun–Fri – except on Jewish holidays – 10am–7pm, winter 10am–5.30pm | museoebraico.it)* where precious Torah shrines, silver candelabras, documents, textiles, furniture and musical instruments bring back to life the rich tradition of Venice's Jewish community. *Tours Sun–Fri (except on Jewish holidays) in Italian and English every hour 10.30am–5.30pm (winter until 4.30pm) | meeting place at the museum | stop: Guglie | ▢ F2–3*

☷ MADONNA DELL'ORTO

An artistic jewel that is unjustly neglected: the brick façade of this Gothic church with its statues of the Apostles and finely carved windows is a feast for the eyes. Inside there are some superb paintings, including *John the Baptist* by Cima da

INSIDER TIP
Hidden treasures

Conegliano and several works by Tintoretto, who is buried in the apse. *Mon–Sat 10am–5pm, Sun noon–5pm | stop: Madonna dell'Orto | ⏱ 45 mins | ▯ H2*

🔟 CHIESA DEI GESUITI

A little bit off the tourist track, on the north-eastern border of Cannaregio, a classic example of Venetian high-Baroque architecture rises into the sky: *Santa Maria Assunta dei Gesuiti*, the main church of the Jesuit Order. The façade, with its colossal columns and intricate sculptural decoration, creates a striking first impression. The painstakingly renovated interior, with its shades of green and white, is even more impressive. Your eyes will be drawn towards the elaborate high altar designed by Giuseppe Pozzo. The most precious decoration, however, is Titian's expressive painting of the *Martyrdom of St Laurentius* in the first chapel of the left-hand nave. *Campo dei Gesuiti | Mon–Fri 10am–noon and 4–7pm, in winter 10am–6pm | stop: Fondamente Nove | ⏱ 30 mins | ▯ K3–4*

🔟 SANTA MARIA DEI MIRACOLI

Fortunately, this pretty Renaissance church was restored in the 1990s. Now its unusual façade with the multi-coloured marble panels can once again be seen at its best. The interior, with its delicate filigree stone masonry throughout, is quite spectacular. *Mon 10.30am–4pm, Tue–Sat 10.30am–4.30pm | stop: Rialto | ⏱ 30 mins | ▯ K5*

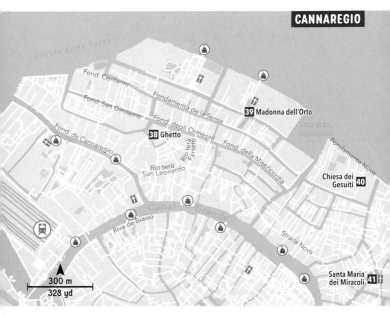

CANNAREGIO

38 Ghetto
39 Madonna dell'Orto
Chiesa dei Gesuiti 40
Santa Maria dei Miracoli 41

300 m
328 yd

SAN POLO & SANTA CROCE

The city started to grow from this core area west of the Rialto Bridge more than 1,000 years ago.

The old trading and banking district on the Canal Grande has hardly lost any of its former bustling character: with its many shops as well as the fish, fruit and vegetable markets, a stroll around here is a feast for the senses. The numerous palaces and churches, first and foremost Santa Maria Gloriosa dei Frari and the neighbouring Scuola Grande di San Rocco, also make it an important hunting ground for art lovers. The best place to watch this hive of activity over a cappuccino or *ombra* – a small glass of wine – is on Campo San Polo, the second largest open space in the city, or in the area between Pescheria and Rialto where many chic shops have breathed new life into the area

42 PONTE DI RIALTO ★

This venerable 16th-century bridge has been given an overhaul which was completed in 2016. Renzo Rosso, founder of jeans label Diesel, generously provided 5 million euros to restore this "bridge of all bridges". Now the 300 steps, almost 400 stone columns and countless paving stones look shiny and fresh. And instead of cheap tat, the shops on the bridge once again sell expensive jewellery, just as they used to: for centuries, this site was the centre of business in the trading metropolis of Venice. It was here that merchants unloaded their goods from faraway lands and the most important banks and trading companies set up their offices. Until the middle of the 19th century, the *Ponte di Rialto* was the only way for pedestrians to cross the Canal Grande. *Stop: Rialto | ⊞ J6*

43 PALAZZO MOCENIGO

Located directly behind Ca' Pesaro and San Stae Church, this magnificent early 17th-century palace, with its furniture, chandeliers, textiles and other decorative objects, gives a good idea of the luxury in which the nobility of the period liked to indulge. A study centre for the history of textiles and fashion has been established in some of its stately rooms. *April–Oct*

Whether you pass over or under it, the Rialto Bridge is not to be missed

Tue–Sun 10.30am–5pm, Nov–March 10am–4pm | stop: San Stae | ⏱ *1½ hrs | 🗺 G4–5*

🟦 CAMPO SAN GIACOMO DELL'ORIO 🐷

INSIDER TIP
Magical moments

A small, quiet place with trees: a rarity in Venice! Plus a 1,000-year-old church. That's quite something! Have a look inside the church of *San Giacomo dell'Orio (Mon–Sat 10.30am–4.30pm)*. After all, it was founded in the ninth century, and then extended several times, always in the style of the prevailing art period at the time. The result is an amusing hotch-potch of styles. Then perhaps indulge in a glass of wine? In good weather, the *Al Prosecco (closed Sun)* wine bar sets up tables outside – lovely! *Stop: Riva di Biasio | 🗺 F5*

🟦 CAMPO SAN POLO

This square is vast, and perfect for a rest – whether free of charge on one of the benches, or over a drink at one of the pretty street cafés. *Stop: San Silvestro | 🗺 G6*

🟦 CASA GOLDONI

The birthplace of playwright Carlo Goldoni, Italy's 18th-century answer to, possibly, Richard Bean. People roared with laughter at his comedies based on the skinflint Pantalone and his scatterbrained manservant Arlecchino. However, his writing did not earn him a fortune, and he had to supplement it by working as a lawyer. Later on, he became an Italian teacher at the

A visit to the 18th-century Casa Goldoni

French court, which should have set him up for life – had it not been for the French Revolution. Goldoni, who is today considered the first representative of modern Italian theatre, died in poverty in Paris in 1793. *Rio Terà dei Nomboli 2794 | April-Oct Thu-Tue noon-5pm, Nov-March 10am-4pm | carlogoldoni.visitmuve.it | stop: San Tomà | ⏱ 30 mins | ☐ G6-7*

47 FRARI ★

Along with the Dominican church of Santi Giovanni e Paolo, the "Frari", as Santa Maria Gloriosa dei Frari is called for short, is the second largest Gothic church of the mendicant orders in the city. In contrast with their self-imposed humility and the building's modest exterior, its commissioners, the Franciscans, did not hold back when it came to the interior. The first thing you will notice in the enormous nave is the pyramidal tomb of Antonio Canova with Titian's grave and his *Pesaro Madonna* opposite. There are delicate altarpieces by Bartolomeo Vivarini and Giovanni Bellini, as well as a statue of *St John* by Donatello in the choir chapels and sacristy where the composer Claudio Monteverdi is also buried.

Most fascinating of all, however, is the painting above the high altar. Titian's floating *Assunta* (Ascension of the Virgin Mary) was a stroke of genius on the part of the artist; its incredible colouring and composition, striving dramatically upwards towards the heavens, were something completely new at the end of the Renaissance and already point towards the Baroque. *Mon-Sat 9am-6pm, Sun 1-6pm | stop: San Tomà | ☐ F6*

48 SCUOLA GRANDE DI SAN ROCCO

If the treasures in this meeting house don't bowl you over, then nothing will! The walls and ceilings of this building dedicated to Saint Roch, who gave protection from the Plague, are decorated with no fewer than 56 paintings, created over a period of 18 years in the late 16th century by Jacopo Robusti, better known as Tintoretto. They show scenes from the

Old and New Testaments. With its perfect proportions and magnificent panelled ceiling, the main hall on the upper floor is considered one of the most exquisite rooms in all of Italy. The adjacent hostel *(Sala dell'Albergo)* with Tintoretto's *Crucifixion* of 1565 is hardly any less impressive. The eight large paintings of the life of the Virgin Mary in the (rather gloomy) entrance hall on the ground floor are also well worth seeing. A few years ago, the *Scoletta di San Rocco (daily 9.30am–6pm)* opposite the *Scuola Grande* opened its doors to visitors. It is quite charming but considerably more modestly decorated and is now used for interesting temporary exhibitions. On no account should you miss *San Rocco Church (daily 9.30am–5.30pm)* next door with its magnificent

Tintoretto paintings. *Daily 9.30am–5.30pm | scuolagrandesanrocco.it | stop: San Tomà | ⏲ 2 hrs | ▱ E–F6*

DORSODURO

Venice's "strong backbone", the sestiere in the south-west of the old city presents itself as a charming mixture of rustic provinciality (during the day) and – thanks to the university nearby – student dynamism (in the evening) on its main square, Campo Santa Margherita, and in its side streets.

The history of Venice as a working city can be seen and felt on its outskirts, especially on the island of Giudecca to the south and in the west

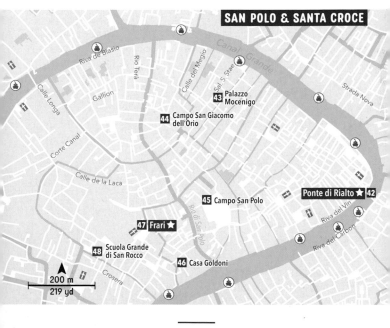

near the harbour – and both areas are part of Dorsoduro. Some parts of the abandoned industrial areas look grim, others as if they were being prepared for a transformation. Venice is also undergoing structural change, and there is a creative scene in need of space. It has it here.

🚩 *Zattere*, the promenade along the Giudecca Canal, is the perfect place to enjoy some sun on a winter walk The view across the water to Palladio's churches is an absolute dream. Art lovers' hearts will start to beat faster further to the east, between the Accademia, the Guggenheim Gallery and Santa Maria della Salute. It is definitely worth making a detour to the monastery island of San Giorgio Maggiore, not only to admire the fantastic panoramic view from the campanile (read more about it in the Palladio walk in the Discovery Tours chapter).

49 SAN PANTALON 🐷🐦

Waiting behind this modest – or one could say, completely blank – façade is a gigantic ceiling painting made up of 40 individual canvas elements that will really turn your head in more ways than one. Gian Antonio Fumiani was the man who worked for 24 years to create this colossal Baroque work at the end of the 17th century. *Mon–Sat 10am–noon and 1–3pm | stop: San Tomà | vw 30 mins | ⌂ E7*

50 CAMPO SANTA MARGHERITA

The long, narrow main square of the Dorsoduro *sestiere* offers a strange mixture: on the one hand, it is probably Venice's most folksy campo – with a fish and vegetable market, wine bars and an everyday lifestyle similar to that in a village. On the other hand, it is in the centre of an extremely lively youth and student scene that has developed in recent years with countless bars, pubs and cabaret theatres between Campo San Pantalon in the north and Rio di San Barnaba in the south.

The Carmelite order's church of *Santa Maria del Carmine (Mon–Sat 7am–noon and 2.30–7pm, Sun 8.30am–noon and 2.30–7pm)* mostly just called Carmini, and its *Scuola Grande dei Carmine (daily 11am–5pm| scuolagrandecarmini.it)*, decorated with paintings by Giambattista Tiepolo, form the south-west end of the *campo*. A beautiful *Adoration of the Shepherds* by Cima da Congeliano (in the second wall altar) and Lorenzo Lotto's *St Nicholas* above the opposite altar can be admired behind the brick façade and threateningly lopsided Baroque campanile. There are also performances of operas in period costumes several times a week *(musica inmaschera.it)*. *Stop: San Basilio, Ca' Rezzonico | ⌂ E7*

51 SAN SEBASTIANO

The hearts of those who admire the cheerful, opulent paintings of Paolo Veronese will beat faster in this church. What, at first glance, appears to be a rather modest church preserves the artistic legacy of this genius. He

The Ponte dei Pugni spans the Rio di San Barnaba in Dorsoduro

painted all the frescoes on the ceilings and walls as well as the high altar and found his final resting place beneath the church's organ. *Mon 10.30am–4pm, Tue–Sat 10.30am–4.30pm | stop: San Basilio | ⏱ 45 mins | ▥ D8*

52 PONTE DEI PUGNI

Until a few years ago, this bridge at Campo San Barnaba was one of only a few without a railing. Now it is more difficult to fall off it into the Rio di San Barnaba. And it's much longer since the end of the spectacle for which it is named: Bridge of Fists. Until into the 16th century, rival factions of the city fought with their fists atop the bridge. The winning team was the one that knocked its opponents off the bridge and into the water. *Stop: Ca' Rezzonico | ▥ E8*

53 GALLERIA DELL'ACCADEMIA ★ ⚑

Bellini, Carpaccio, Giorgione, Tintoretto, Titian and Veronese, Canaletto, Longhi, Mantegna, Lotto, Piazzetta and Tiepolo… There is hardly a single prominent representative of the more than 500-year history of Venetian painting who has not found a place in this museum on the southern bank of the Canal Grande. It is no wonder that this art gallery is considered one of the most important in the world. Don't be put off by the long queues of visitors that sometimes line up in front of the neoclassical façade: it is well worth waiting to see what is on display in the two dozen rooms of the spacious complex of buildings that was developed out of the former church, monastery and Scuola della

Carità. If you do not want to wait too long, you can book a fixed time in advance *(tel. 04 15 20 03 45)* at an extra charge of 1.50 euros.

If you don't want to spend half a day in the museum, have a look at the following highlights: Gentile Bellini's *Miracle of the Relic of the Cross*, Vittore Carpaccio's *Legend of St Ursula* cycle, Giorgione's *The Tempest* and *Old Woman*, various Old Testament scenes and portraits of saints by Tintoretto and Paolo Veronese, as well as scenes of everyday life by Pietro Longhi, landscapes and views of cities by Canaletto and Francesco Guardi. And finally, Tiziano Vecellio, alias Titian: this giant among the masters of the Renaissance is represented with a wonderful painting of *John the Baptist*, his last work, *Pietà*, and *The Presentation of the Virgin Mary*, the only painting by Titian that is still in the place it was intended for. *Tue–Sun 8.15am–7.15pm, Mon 8.15am–2pm | gallerieaccademia.it | stop: Accademia | ⏱ 2 hrs | ▥ F9*

🟥 PONTE DELL'ACCADEMIA

When it was erected in 1932, this wooden bridge was planned to be a temporary replacement for its predecessor that was too low for *vaporetto* traffic. But, as is often the case with interim solutions, the Venetians have become used to it and no longer want to be without it when they – and all of the visitors from far and near – admire the wonderful view down the canal towards Salute and, in the opposite direction, to Palazzo Balbi at the mouth of the Rio Foscari. *Stop: Accademia | ▥ F–G 8–9*

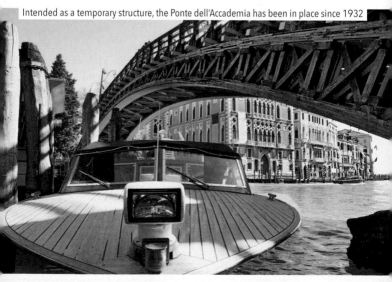

Intended as a temporary structure, the Ponte dell'Accademia has been in place since 1932

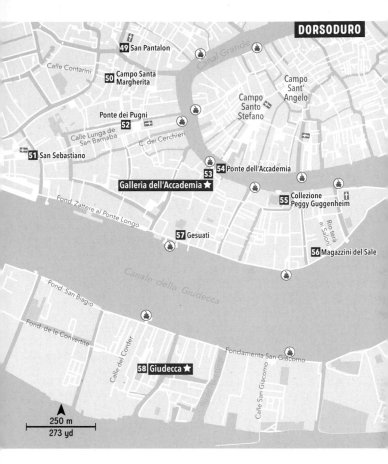

55 COLLEZIONE PEGGY GUGGENHEIM 🎏

Cubism and Surrealism, Action Painting and abstract art – there is no movement in classical modern art that Peggy Guggenheim, a rich heiress and patron of the arts, did not collect in her Palazzo Venier dei Leoni. The low building has become a mecca for lovers of 20th-century art. Among the great painters and sculptors on display here are Joan Mirò, René Magritte, Henri Matisse, Henry Moore, Piet Mondrian, Wassily Kandinsky, Georges Braque, Paul Klee, Jackson Pollock and many, many more. The museum shop sells fabulous posters and art books, writing accessories and postcards – it's a great place to browse! *Wed–Mon 10am–6pm | guggenheim-venice.it | stop: Accademia, Salute |* ⏱ *1½ hrs |* 🗺 *G9*

56 MAGAZZINI DEL SALE

This is the newest and most modern museum in the district, housed in what was once a salt store. On display are works by the celebrated abstract expressionist Emilio Vedova, who died in 2006. As space is limited, architect Renzo Piano – who was a friend of Vedova – came up with something really special: the works are changed by automation several times a day. *Fondamenta Zattere 50 | Wed–Sun 10.30am–6pm | fondazione vedova.org | stop: Spirito Santo | ⌂ H10*

INSIDER TIP
A changing exhibition

57 GESUATI

On your stroll along the picturesque Zattere quay, it is worth taking some time to visit this sacred building designed by the great Venetian architect of the Baroque period, Giorgio Massari. Inside you can admire the beautiful ceiling frescos by Giambattista Tiepolo and altarpieces by Tintoretto, Giovanni Battista Piazzetta and Sebastiano Ricci. *Mon–Sat 10.30am–4.30pm | stop: Zattere | ⌂ F9*

58 GIUDECCA ★

This island to the south of the old city is actually made up of eight smaller ones connected to each other. In the Middle Ages, this was the home of the Jews – *guidei* (from which the name probably stems) – who had been expelled from the city. Later, rich Venetians built their summer villas here, followed, in the 19th century, by trade and industry. Today, the main reason for visiting this area of the city, which is under the administration of the Dorsoduro *sestiere*, is to see Palladio's two churches: Redentore and Zitelle. Well-heeled guests book into the five-star Cipriani Hotel on the eastern tip. The former Molino Stucky grain mill in the west, which partially burned down in 2003, has come back to life as a luxurious Hilton Hotel. Stops: *Zitelle, Redentore, Palanca | ⌂ C–K 10–12*

THE ISLANDS

No exploration of Venice would be complete without visiting at least two or three of the islands off the coast of the centro storico.

The view over the lagoon 👁 alone makes the trip on the *vaporetto* an unforgettable experience. The small island of Murano is only 15 minutes away by boat and a visit to it and one of its glass-blowing workshops is a classic. On the way, you can stop off at San Michele, the cemetery island. Further to the north-east are Burano, famous for its lacework, and Sant'Erasmo.

59 SAN SERVOLO

10 mins with line 20 from San Zaccaria

This tiny island near the Lido was once the accommodation for the *pazzi clamorosi*, the "dangerously deluded". The psychiatric facility was closed in 1978, and the island was abandoned. Today it is possible to visit the

INSIDER TIP
Not for the faint-hearted

old *manicomio*, the psychiatric ward, and find out more about the hair-raising treatments used on the mentally ill at the *Museo del Manicomio (Mon–Fri 10.45am and 2pm | museo manicomio.servizimetropolitani.ve.it | ⏱ 1 hr)*. Please be aware that strait-jackets and electric shock therapy were regarded as the gentlest methods! *Stop: San Servolo |* 🚌 *0*

🚌 LIDO 👫

15 mins with line 1 from San Zaccaria
This 12-km-long and 200- to 1,700-m-wide strip of sand protects the city from storms and flooding. Since the 19th century, it has also served the Venetians as a place to spend their leisure time and for guests from abroad as a seaside resort. In the early days of tourism, mainly the nobility, the rich and powerful of Europe, as well as privileged artists, enjoyed the *dolce far niente* on the fine sand of the Lido's beach. The splendid villas, hotels and parks are evidence of this. The loveliest is the Grand Hotel des Bains, built in 1900 and the inspiration behind Thomas Mann's *Death in Venice*. Luchino Visconti's fabulous film of this novella takes place here, and *The English Patient* was also filmed at the Des Bains. The end came in 2010. The hotel was closed, and since then has been slowly crumbling away behind a high corrugated-steel fence. There were plans for a group of investors to convert it into luxury apartments, and now there is also talk of it re-opening as a hotel, but this could take time. At least the 1930s *Palazzo del Cinema* has been restored and a hall added. Venice's glamorous film festival is held here each year at the beginning of September.

The aristocratic flair has largely vanished, but the atmosphere and infrastructure for carefree seaside

Beach life on the Lido

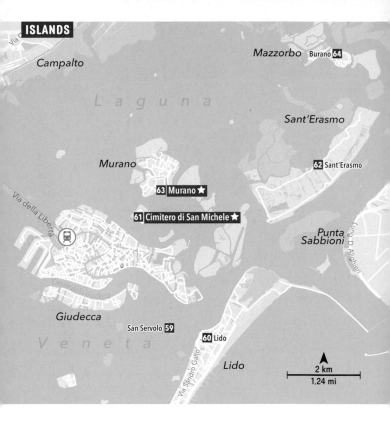

holidays have remained. There are well cared-for beaches with inviting pizzerias, ice cream parlours and bars waiting for sun worshippers and keen swimmers within walking distance of the main road Viale Santa Maria Elisabetta. Night-owls will find several clubs; for sports enthusiasts there are rowing and sailing clubs; and if you want to get on your bike, there is a network of cycle tracks all over the Lido and the neighbouring island of Pellestrina to the south. It is worth visiting the old Jewish cemetery near the northern tip of the Lido, the *Antico Cimitero Ebraico (April–Oct by appointment | tel. 0 41 71 53 59)* and, not far away, the *Aeroporto Nicelli*, an architectural gem in the Bauhaus style. Those who are interested can take the ferry from Ca' Roman, a small conservation area in the south-west, to the mainland and then travel by bus or – even better – by bike (rental at the Lido *vaporetto* stop, *lidoonbike.it*) to Chioggia. Strictly speaking, this colourful, lively fishing town does not belong to Venice and is more oriented towards the mainland and the sea than the lagoon. *Stops: Lido, San Nicolò | 📖 0*

61 CIMITERO DI SAN MICHELE ★ 🐾

6 mins with line 4.1 or 4.2 from Fondamente Nove

Venice's cemetery island is situated halfway to Murano. Thousands of anonymous Venetians have been laid to rest under the cypresses behind the brick walls, as have some prominent visitors from abroad including the composer Igor Stravinsky, the poet Ezra Pound and the great Russian ballet impresario Sergei Diaghilev. *Daily 7.30am–6pm (in winter until 4pm) | stop: Cimitero | 🚏 M–N 1–3*

62 SANT'ERASMO

28 mins with line 13 from Fondamente Nove

Sant'Erasmo, measuring 4.4km long and 1.2km wide, is Venice's kitchen garden. Rare lilac artichokes grow here, as does green, very thin asparagus. You can stroll along the virtually traffic-free road that circles the island, and through the fields and meadows that are irrigated by narrow canals. Or borrow a bike from *Il Lato Azzurro (Via dei Forti 13 | latoazzurro.it)*, a co-operative that also runs a basic hotel and restaurant on the island.

Be sure to visit the *Orto di Venezia* vineyard *(Via delle Motte 1 | ortodivenezia. com)* which belongs to a determined Frenchman who was the first person to reintroduce wine growing to the island. After that, take a (swimming) break at the Spiaggia del Bacan at the south-western tip of the island. Stop: Capannone | 🚏 0

> **INSIDER TIP**
> **Wine from the garden isle**

63 MURANO ★

10 mins with line 4.1, 4.2 or 13 from Fondamente Nove

Comprising five islands and inhabited for around 1,400 years, this community (pop. today: almost 7,000) is famous for its glass industry. Make sure you visit one of the workshops as well as the *Museo del Vetro (daily 10am–6pm, in winter until 5pm | stop: Museo)*. With more than 4,000 exhibits, this museum documents the 1,000-year history of glass-blowing on Murano. Of particular interest to art lovers are the Romanesque former *Santi Maria e Donato Cathedral (Mon–Sat 9am–6pm, Sun 12.30–6pm)*, with its two-storey arcades in the choir section and original mosaic floor, and the *San Pietro Martire Church (Mon–Fri 9am–5.30pm, Sat/Sun noon–5.30pm)*, which houses one of Giovanni Bellini's major works. *Various stops | 🚏 P–S 1–4*

64 BURANO 🚩

42 mins with line 12 from Fondamente Nove

Everything is smaller and more colourful here than in Venice. The island, which is world famous for its embroidered lace *(merletti)*, is a great mood lifter with the brightly coloured façades of the houses. The prettiest one is *Casa di Bepi Suà*, whose unconventional owners have painted it in all sorts of patterns. If there's still time after a walk and a drink, then visit the *Museo del Merletto (Tue–Sun 10am–5pm, in summer until 6pm)*. *Stop: Burano | ⏱ 1 hr | 🚏 W–X 1–2*

EATING & DRINKING

It is generally easy to eat well at fair prices anywhere in Italy, but sadly not in Venice. This is because many restaurants make so much money from day-trippers, who most likely will never return, that it really doesn't matter whether the customers were satisfied with the food or not.

Of course, there are chefs who use fresh produce from the lagoon's vegetable islands and its rich marine environment to serve magical creative cuisine, but this comes at a price. You have to ask yourself whether it's worth saving your cash and putting up with an

There is always time for a spritz in Venice

unappetising *menù turistico* at exorbitant rates. In our opinion, it's not! Much better to pay more for your food and get to know Venice's true culinary delicacies.

These include pickled sardines, pasta with clams, as well as dried cod cooked in a creamy milky stock. If your budget is running low, you can still visit the many *bacari* (the initial "a" being stressed) which serve titbits with your glass of wine, often free of charge or for just a few euros. These Venetian tapas are called *cicchetti*, and as a snack they are a thousand times better than fast food.

WHERE TO EAT IN VENICE

Laguna Veneta

FONDAMENTA DELLA MISERICORDIA
Small wine bars and nice osterias in Cannaregio

Sant' Alvise

Madonna dell'Orto

Fondamenta San Girolamo

Fondamenta de la Sensa

Fond. degli Ormesini

Fondamenta de Cannaregio

Fondamente Nove

Fond. de la Misericordia

Guglie

Gam-Gam ★

Strada Nova

Riva de Biasio

Venezia Santa Lucia

S. Stae

Ca' d'Oro

Strada Nova

AROUND CA' D'ORO
Cosy bacari and rustic cuisine

AROUND THE RIALTO MARKET
Move from one hip bar to the next, tasting all kinds of goodies

Do Mori ★

Rialto Mercato

Naranzaria ★

Riva del Vin

Rialto

Riva del Carbon

Crosera

C. Contarini

Piazza San Marco

Campo Santo Stefano

San Marco

Bacino

FONDAMENTA MANIN ON MURANO

A selection of fish restaurants for all budgets

Museo

Rivalonga

Fondamenta Venier

C. Brussa

Fondamenta Antonio Maschio

Fondamenta Manin

Colonna

Cimitero di San Michele

Canali delle Fondamenta Nuova

Fondamente Nove

Canale Grande

Darsena Grande

Corte Sconta ★

Riva degli Schiavoni

Arsenale

di San Marco

Via Giuseppe Garibaldi

250 m
273 yd

MARCO POLO HIGHLIGHTS

★ **DO MORI**
Treat yourself to a glass of wine in Venice's oldest wine bar ➤ p.68

★ **NARANZARIA**
In this gourmet restaurant, it is possible to sit right on the Canal Grande until late at night ➤ p.68

★ **CORTE SCONTA**
Wonderful fish dishes in a local atmosphere ➤ p.71

★ **GAM-GAM**
Now, here's something different: kosher cuisine and Israeli wines ➤ p.75

Regardless of whether you eat in a gourmet restaurant or trattoria, the classical menu is always the same: you begin with starters *(antipasti)*, followed by soup, pasta or risotto as the *primo piatto* (first course). The main course *(secondo piatto)* consists of fish or meat with a vegetable or salad side dish *(contorno)*, which must be ordered separately. All of this concludes with a dessert *(dolce)* and/or fruit. This is usually accompanied by wine *(vino)*, often the house wine *(della casa)* with a carafe of water to quench your thirst.

The kitchens are usually open from noon until around 2.30pm for lunch, and from 7pm to around 10pm in the evening. There is almost always an extra cover charge *(pane e coperto)* of 1–3 euros (sometimes more); this includes bread to go with your meal. It will say on the menu if the service charge *(servizio)* is included; if not, a tip of five to ten percent is appropriate – as long as you were satisfied.

BACARI, BARS & OSTERIE

Locals meet up in simply furnished but welcoming wine bars in order to knock back a few tasty morsels *(cicchetti)* while standing at the bar, or to enjoy a hearty meal seated at a table in an osteria. Either way, the food is accompanied by an *ombra*, the small glass of white wine that is considered an essential part of daily life in Venice.

DA ALBERTO

Could it be more Venetian? We think not. Alberto serves typical dishes such as *sarde in saor*, pickled sardines, and *baccalà mantecato*, dried cod cooked in milk and stock until wonderfully creamy, that are just as the Venetians makes them at home. *Daily | Calle Giacinto Gallina 5401 | tel. 04 15 23 81 53 | osteriadaalberto.it | stop: Ospedale | Castello | ⧄ L5*

AMERICAN BAR

Although you can't sit down, the location right below the clock tower on St Mark's Square is unbeatable, the selection of sandwiches and drinks is excellent, and the prices – especially compared to the wickedly expensive posh cafés in the area – are pleasantly moderate. Plus, you can still enjoy the unique panorama of the square and the sun at the standing tables outside. *Daily | stop: San Marco | San Marco | ⧄ K7*

ANTICO CALICE

Located right around the corner from the lively Campo San Bartolomeo, this storybook Osteria serves up an incredible selection of classic specialities and good wines to a mixed crowd of young locals and tourists in equal measure. *Daily | Calle dei Stagneri 5228 | tel. 04 15 20 97 75 | antico calice.it | stop: Rialto | Rialto | ⧄ J6*

CANTINE DEL VINO GIÀ SCHIAVI

The chef of this long-established *bacaro* has created 70 recipes for *cicchetti*, and every morning she freshly prepares about 50 or so: classics such as dried cod cream, but also sweet-and-sour combinations. There are no chairs, but it is truly romantic to

The Naranzaria serves sushi and sashimi fresh from the fish market next door

INSIDER TIP
"Cheers" on the bridge

sit down on the steps of the bridge opposite with a well-cooled glass of pinot grigio and a plate of delicious food. *Closed Sun and from 8.30pm | Fondamenta Nani 992 | tel. 04 15 23 00 34 | cantinaschiavi.com | stop: Accademia | Accademia | ⚹ F9*

ENOTECA LA MASCARETA

The not-quite-successful shabby chic interior and eccentric owner add an entertainment value to the place. The

INSIDER TIP
Sustenance for night owls

choice of wines is excellent, and as well as serving snacks, you can also get a hearty something for your hunger when it's late.

Closed at lunchtime | Calle Lunga Santa Maria Formosa 5183 | tel.

04 15 23 07 44 | ostemaurolorenzon. com | stop: Ospedale | Castello | ⚹ L6

HOSTARIA OSOTTOOSOPRA

Here several friends have realised their dream of opening a restaurant with a cosy atmosphere and good food. The wooden ceiling beams and unplastered walls give the interior a special flair, the starters are refined, the pasta in a truffle sauce and the glazed beef cheeks are delicious. 🐷 If you book online, you get a 20% discount! *Daily | Calle San Pantalon 5754 I tel. 33 38 02 78 30 | osottoosopra. com | stop: San Tomà | Frari | ⚹ E7*

AL MERCÀ

A pick-me-up in the open air on a peaceful square near Rialto Bridge: tasty unusual canapés with horsemeat, cauliflower, dried cod or tuna… Good local wine. *Closed Sun | Fondamenta Riva Olio 213 | tel. 39 39 92 47 81 | stop: Rialto | Rialto | ▥ J5*

DO MORI ★

Icon – the oldest *bacaro* in Venice. Serving wine (over 100 labels!) and snacks for more than 500 years. The *tramezzini* are delicious. You simply must see it. Unfortunately, because it is now so well-known, it is also over-priced: just close your eyes, and get through it. *Closed Sun and from 8.30pm | Calle dei Do Mori 429 | tel. 04 15 22 54 01 | stop: Rialto | Rialto | ▥ H5–6*

NARANZARIA ★

This classy pub in the new trendy quarter between the fish market and Rialto Bridge serves spicy snacks as well as main dishes ranging from carpaccio to couscous, from polenta to pasta, and even sushi, accompanied by excellent wines from Friuli. If the weather is fine, you can sit outside on the Canal Grande until long past midnight. *Nov–March closed Mon| Sotoportego de l'Erbaria 130 | tel. 04 17 24 10 35 | naranzaria.it | stop: Rialto Mercato | Rialto | ▥ J5*

OSTERIA BANCOGIRO

Join the action at the fish market when the offices close and young Venetians come here to enjoy the evening with Aperol spritz or prosecco.

This small, very popular osteria serves the most delicious *cicchetti*, which are eaten while standing, cheek to cheek with local people. *Closed Mon | Campo San Giacometto 122 | tel. 04 15 23 20 61 | osteriabancogiro.it | stop: Rialto | Rialto | ▥ J5–6*

LA RIVISTA

Stylish wine-and-cheese bar in the cellar of the design hotel Ca' Pisani. Tasty cold food and small warm dishes, excellent range of wines. *Closed Mon | Rio Terà Foscarini 979 | tel. 04 12 40 14 25 | stop: Accademia, Zattere | Accademia | ▥ F9*

TEAMO

Delicacies in a stylish ambiance – great for a tasty snack or a good chat with a glass of wine or a cocktail. Tip: the mixed *cicchetti* platter. *Closed Thu | Rio Terà della Mandola 3795 | tel. 04 15 28 37 87 | teamowinebar. com | stop: Sant'Angelo | San Marco | ▥ H7*

TRATTORIA DALLA MARISA 🍖

There is no carte, only a set menu of the day, but this is worth it: three start-ers, pasta, a main course (meat or fish), dessert – wow! It is no wonder that builders, boatsmen as well as the odd count come here for lunch. Everybody is sitting cheek to cheek and the atmosphere, while being rough, is refreshingly genuine. *Closed Mon evening and Tue evening | Calle Canna 652b/Fondamenta San Giobbe | tel. 0 41 72 02 11 | stop: Tre Archi | Cannaregio | ▥ D2*

VECIO FRITOLIN

Very traditional osteria, full of atmos-phere, perfect for a good meal or just a

Today's Specials

Antipasti

CARPACCIO
Wafer-thin slices of raw beef, with a trickle of lemon juice and flakes of Parmesan

SARDE IN SAOR
Cooked sardines served cold with a marinade of olive oil, vinegar, wine, raisins and pine nuts

FOLPETTI ALLA VENEZIANA
Cooked baby octopus

FIORI DI ZUCCA
Pumpkin flowers, usually served stuffed and fried

Primi Piatti

BIGOLI IN SALSA
Spaghetti with anchovy sauce

RISI E BISI
Rice with green peas

RISOTTO NERO
Creamy black risotto prepared with squid ink *(seppie)*

BROETO
Creamy smooth fish soup

PASTA E FAGIOLI
A substantial stew cooked with thick macaroni, white beans and a lot of olive oil

Secondi Piatti

BACCALÀ MANTECATO
A paste made of mashed dried cod, garlic, onions and olive oil

FRITTO MISTO DI MARE
Fried fish and seafood

CAPESANTE GRATINATE
Gratinated scallops

CANOCE AL VAPORE
Steamed mantis shrimp

FEGATO ALLA VENEXIANA
Calf's liver cooked in a white wine and onion stock

Dolci

FRITOLE
Roundish sweet fritters made from dough with raisins and pine nuts

GALANI
A traditional Carnival sweet: wafer-thin dough ribbons dusted with icing sugar

few savoury *cicchetti*. Delicious fish dishes! *Closed Wed lunchtime and Tue | Calle della Regina 2262 | tel. 04 15 22 28 81 | veciofritolin.it | stop: San Stae | San Polo | ⬜ H5*

CAFÉS & ICE CREAM PARLOURS

ALASKA

This is the most unusual – and probably the smallest – *gelateria* in the city. They make dozens of exotic and unusual flavours of ice cream from natural ingredients, ranging from asparagus and ginger or artichoke and liquorice to mulberry. Pure bliss! *Daily 11am–11pm, in winter noon–10pm, closed Dec/Jan | Calle Larga dei Bari 1159 | stop: Ferrovia, Riva de Biasio | Cannaregio | ⬜ F5*

CAFFÈ DEL DOGE

A paradise for caffeine *aficionados* with dozens of coffee varieties. The beans are freshly ground, which smells just wonderful. Close to the Rialto Bridge, but slightly hidden down an alley. *Mon–Sat 7am–7pm, Sun (except July/Aug) 7am–1pm | Calle dei Cinque 609 | stop: San Silvestro, Rialto | Rialto | ⬜ J6*

IMAGINA CAFÈ

A great port of call at any time of day or night, for a cappuccino, a quick snack at lunchtime or a cocktail in the evening. Modern design and changing exhibitions by contemporary artists. *Mon–Thu 7am–9pm, Fri/Sat 7am–1pm, Sun 8am–9pm | Rio Terà Canal 3126 | tel. 04 12 41 06 25 | imaginacafe.it | stop: Ca' Rezzonico | Dorsoduro | ⬜ E8*

Have you ever tried artichoke or ginger flavours? The Alaska sells amazing ice cream.

TORREFAZIONE CANNAREGIO
Everyone knows the Florian on St Mark's Square, and this historic coffee house in Cannaregio is just as iconic – with the locals. The prices are normal, and the aroma of the freshly-ground coffee is – wow! *Closed in the evenings | Fondamenta dei Ormesini 2804 | torrefazionecannaregio.it | stop: Sant'Alvise | Cannaregio | ⬚ F–G2*

RESTAURANTS €€€

ACQUASTANCA
The two women who run this minimalist-modern restaurant really know their business. Fabulously prepared starters (octopus salad, crispy fried *gamberoni*, creamy dried cod) and the fish dishes are full of flair. *Closed Sun and evenings except Mon and Fri | Fondamenta Manin 48 | tel. 04 13 19 51 25 | acquastanca.it | stop: Murano | Murano | ⬚ Q3*

LA CARAVELLA
The décor may be questionable and rather kitsch, but it is a nautical theme after all, and a Captain's Dinner is something different (as well as pricey ...). The waiters are highly attentive, making sure that your glass is always filled, and demonstrate the professionalism which you would expect from the luxury hotel to which the restaurant belongs. In good weather you should book a table in their romantic garden! *Daily | Calle Larga XXII Marzo 2399 | tel. 04 15 20 89 01 | restaurantlacaravella. com | stop: Giglio | San Marco | ⬚ H8*

INSIDER TIP
Al fresco dinner

CORTE SCONTA ★
This modestly furnished restaurant is not easy to find but you will be rewarded with an excellent selection of first-class fish. The specials of the day are not listed on the menu but rattled off by the lady of the house in Italian. Don't despair, just mention which fish or sea fruit you would like or see what your neighbours have ordered: you are bound to get a lovely dish. The opulent plate of *antipasti* is recommended, but be aware that quality has its price! *Closed Sun/ Mon. | Calle del Pestrin 3886 | tel. 04 15 22 70 24 | cortescontavenezia. com | stop: Arsenale | Arsenale | ⬚ N8*

DA FIORE
Have you had enough of the fish and seafood? This luxury restaurant serves an enormous selection of Italian cheeses from fresh, aged and strongly scented to spicy. Therefore, you should leave sufficient space for a cheese platter – and afterwards for their superb fruit sorbet or another great dessert. By the way, they also serve fish. *Closed Sun/Mon | Calle del Scaleter 2202 | tel. 0 41 72 13 08 | dafiore.net | stop: San Stae, San Silvestro | San Polo | ⬚ G5*

AI GONDOLIERI
Wonderful 1940s ambience with dark wood, heavy cutlery, fine tablecloths: this is where Humphrey Bogart would have taken Ingrid Bergman for dinner. A specialty are their white truffle dishes. The adjoining wine store has marvellous wines. *Daily | Calle San Domenico 366 | tel. 04 15 28 63 96 |*

aigondolieri.it | stop: Salute | Accademia | ᴔ G9

IL RIDOTTO

This restaurant, with its brick walls and mirrors and elegant atmosphere, only has enough room for a maximum of 13 guests. Gianni Bonaccorsi serves his guests culinary highlights of supreme quality. *Closed Thu lunchtime and Wed | Campo Santi Filippo e Giacomo 4509 | tel. 04 15 20 82 80 | ilridotto.com | stop: San Zaccaria | San Marco | ᴔ L7*

RESTAURANTS €€

ANDRI

Everything is just right here: the freshly prepared food, the reasonable prices, the modern ambience in warm hues, and owner Luca's heartfelt friendliness. A creative mind. His large-scale pictures hang on the walls, and he also designed the hand-blown water glasses himself. Come for the second time, and you'll be welcomed like a regular. *Closed Mon/Tue | Via Lepanto 21 | tel. 04 15 26 54 82 | stop: Lido | Lido | ᴔ 0*

DA CHERUBINO

You have just completed the sightseeing marathon in St Mark's quarter, are feeling really hungry and can't bear the thought of walking any further? Then you are in the right place! Despite the proximity to St Mark's Square, here they don't rip off the tourists, but treat them as valued customers. The spaghetti with octopus are particularly good as well as all of

their seafood. *Closed Sun in winter | Calle Frezzeria San Marco 1702 | tel. 04 15 22 15 43 | stop: San Marco | San Marco | ᴔ J7*

LOCAL

Stylish and pleasant: this is the young and modern Venice. Chef Matteo grew up in Burano where he learned fishing from his father and cooking from his mother. Matteo has known the farmers who supply him with fruit and vegetables since childhood. His specialties include the purple artichokes from Sant'Erasmo island. The kitchen is open to view so that you can watch Matteo and his team prepare the food. *Closed Wed lunchtime | Salizzada dei Greci 3303 | tel. 04 12 41 11 28 | ristorantelocal.com | stop: San Zaccaria | San Zaccaria | ᴔ M7*

LINEA D'OMBRA

Creative cooking focussing on sophisticated fish dishes and a list of more than 600 (!) wines draw people to this smartly designed restaurant. Unforgettable: a meal or an 🦐 aperitif on the pontoon terrace over the water. *Closed Wed | Zattere/Ponte dell'Umiltà 19 | tel. 04 12 41 18 81 | ristorantelineadombra.com | stop: Salute | Giudecca | ᴔ H10*

OGIO

Hold on, it's going to get kitschy now. What could be better than dinner by candlelight inside ancient monastic ruins? Pop the question here, and she's sure to say yes. Even the food (fish, meat, vegetarian) is good, but that's actually a minor matter. *Closed*

Anice Stellato: sit by the canal in Cannaregio and feast on *frutti di mare*

Mon evening and Sun | Campo dei Gesuiti 4877 | tel. 0 41 24 11 12 27 | stop: Fondamente Nove | *Cannaregio* | ▦ *K4*

OSTERIA ANICE STELLATO

"In" establishment with yuppie thirty-somethings, and therefore lots of suits and ties. And yet the atmosphere is relaxed and friendly. The fish and sea-food dishes have already won a Gambero Rosso award. *Closed Sun/ Mon | Fondamenta della Sensa 3272 | tel. 0 41 72 07 44 | osterianicestellato. com | stop: Sant'Alvise | Cannaregio |* ▦ *G2*

OSTERIA DA RIOBA

The best home-made pasta in the city – and of course, fish in every possible

variation. Most of the vegetables come from Sant'Erasmo. Creative cuisine, but not too outlandish. *Closed Mon | Fondamenta della Misericordia 2553 | tel. 04 15 24 43 79 | darioba. com | stop: San Marcuola | Cannaregio |* ▦ *H3*

OSTERIA DI SANTA MARINA

Here you don't get the usual food, but dishes with flair. The vegetables are sourced from the lagoon's islands and the pasta and pastries are home-made. To those who like to try a greater variety, we rec-ommend their tasting menu. And if you find yourself unable to decide, just ask the nice waiters for advice. *Closed Mon lunchtime and*

INSIDER TIP
A little bit of everything

Sun | Campo Santa Marina 5911 | tel. 04 15 28 52 39 | osteriadisantamarina. com | stop: Rialto | Rialto | ⊞ K6

LA PALANCA
Andrea used to be a manager in Milan – now he runs his own restaurant on Giudecca island with great enthusiasm and is always keen to talk. The practical aspect is that this establishment is directly by the ferry stop. It is cosy inside and a dream outside due to its location on the promenade by the Canale della Giudecca. The

The Ghimel Garden in the ghetto serves kosher cuisine

swordfish carpaccio is sliced thinly to perfection and the stuffed ravioli are home-made. Ask the waiter for the recommended main course because they often serve freshly caught fish which isn't listed on the menu. Try the delicious titbits with your aperitif. Afterwards Andrea goes home because the restaurant is closed in the evening. *Closed Sun and evenings | Fondamenta Sant'Eufemia 448 | tel. 04 15 28 77 19 | stop: Palanca | San Marco | ⊞ E–F11*

ALLA VECCHIA PESCHERIA
An old factory warehouse on Murano decorated with stylish furnishings and contemporary art. Picturesque terrace with a fountain. The menu features creative gourmet dishes made from local organic products farmed on the nearby vegetable islands as well as fish and *dolce alla mamma*. *Closed Wed | Campiello Pescheria 4 | tel. 04 15 27 49 57 | allavecchiapescheria. com | stop: Colonna | Murano | ⊞ Q3*

VINI DA GIGIO
Seasonal cuisine with lots of Venetian classics. Regulars also appreciate the value for money – so be sure to book in advance. *Closed Mon/Tue | Fondamenta San Felice 3628a | tel. 04 15 28 51 40 | vinidagigio.com | stop: Ca' d'Oro | Cannaregio | ⊞ J4*

RESTAURANTS €

BANDIERETTE
Good, home-style cooking – something that simple is a rarity in Venice these days. At noon, local workers

drop in, whereas in the evening it is families and groups of friends. Generous servings. No wonder that it will be hard to find a table if you haven't reserved. *Closed Mon evening and Tue | Barbaria de le Tole 6671 | tel. 04 15 22 06 19 | stop: Ospedale | Castello | ⏥ M6*

CANTINA DO SPADE

Ultra-cosy, tasty, value for money – eat your way down the menu. Typical Venetian cuisine. *Closed Tue lunchtime | Calle delle Spade 860 | tel. 04 15 21 05 83 | cantinadospade. com | stop: Rialto | Rialto | ⏥ H5*

DUE COLONNE

A small and bright restaurant with fabulous pizza as well as good meat dishes. In fine weather book a table outside in the square! *Closed Mon | Campo Sant'Agostin 2343 | tel. 0 41 71 73 38 | stop: San Silvestro, San Stae | San Polo | ⏥ G5*

FANTÀSIA

The restaurant is run by young disabled people. The service can be a bit slow at times, so please be patient, but the pasta, risotti and fish dishes are really good. *Closed Mon | Calle Crosera 3911 | tel. 04 15 22 80 38 | ristorantepizzeria.venezia.it | stop: Arsenale | Arsenale | ⏥ N8*

GAM-GAM ★

Kosher cooking in the Jewish-Italian tradition: falafel, gefilte fish and Mediterranean recipes accompanied by excellent Israeli wines. *Closed Fri evening and Sat lunchtime |*

Sotoportego del Gheto Vecchio 1122 | tel. 04 12 75 92 56 | gamgamkosher. com | stop: Guglie | Ghetto | ⏥ F3

GHIMEL GARDEN

What does a shabbat evening in the ancient ghetto look like? The answer is: all you can eat! Experience the typical shabbat menu of kosher dishes on Friday evening or Saturday lunchtime in an incredible garden and lovely atmosphere. Booking required. *Daily | Campo del Ghetto Nuovo | tel. 04 12 43 07 11 | ghimelgarden.com | stop: San Marcuola | Ghetto | ⏥ F2*

OSTERIA AL MERCÀ

Just a few *cicchetti* with your wine or the full works – the choice is yours. The emphasis is on fish. Little wonder – the osteria is located where the old fish market used to be. Beautifully refurbished, with a conservatory. *Daily | Via Dandolo 17 | tel. 04 12 43 16 63 | osteriaalmerca.it | stop: Lido | Lido | ⏥ 0*

TRATTORIA ALLA RAMPA

Spartan ambience in one of the few unspoilt parts of the city. Hardly any tourists ever come here. But lots of workers and *gondolieri* do. Large portions, small prices, unfortunately only open at lunchtime. *Closed Sat/ Sun and evenings | Via Garibaldi 1135 | tel. 04 15 28 53 65 | stop: Giardini | Garibaldi | ⏥ P9*

SHOPPING

It can be hard to avoid the travelling salesmen selling plastic gondolas made in China, and the shop windows full of cheap souvenirs. In Venice you need patience and the right addresses to shop for beautiful items; it is possible but expensive.

A hand-made mask comes at a price, as does hand-dipped and marbled paper or a mouth-blown Murano vase, but these are treasured items that you can only find here in Venice. Browsing the artisan shops and workshops is an experience in itself. In this way, you will not only get to know Venice intimately, but your custom also contributes

Modern, colourful, original: contemporary glass art in Murano

to making sure that the city doesn't end up as yet another Disneyland. Spontaneous shoppers and browsers come to *Le Mercerie*, Venice's main shopping street. The area between the Rialto Bridge and St Mark's Square has countless boutiques, jewellery shops, leather goods and shoes, as well as small glass and artisan workshops.

On work days, the shops usually open their doors between 9am and 10am and close at 12.30 or 1pm for a siesta. They open again from 2.30pm or 3pm until 7pm or 7.30pm. Many shops remain closed on Monday morning.

WHERE TO SHOP IN VENICE

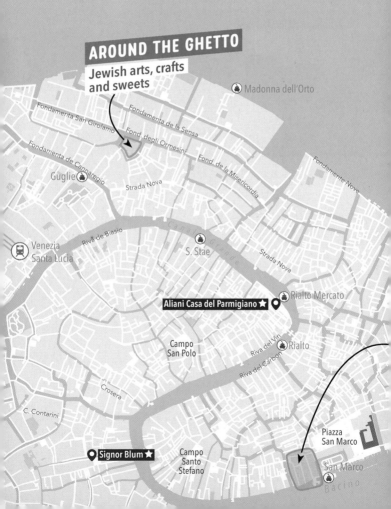

FONDAMENTA DEI VETRAI ON MURANO

Galleries and showrooms full of glass artworks and designer items

AROUND THE GHETTO

Jewish arts, crafts and sweets

Madonna dell'Orto

Fondamenta San Girolamo

Fondamenta de la Sensa

Fond. degli Ormesini

Fond. de la Misericordia

Fondamenta de Cannaregio

Fondamente Nove

Guglie

Strada Nova

Riva de Biasio

Venezia Santa Lucia

S. Stae

Strada Nova

Aliani Casa del Parmigiano ★

Rialto Mercato

Campo San Polo

Riva del Vin

Rialto

Riva del Carbon

Crosera

C. Contarini

Piazza San Marco

Signor Blum ★

Campo Santo Stefano

San Marco

Bacino

MARCO POLO HIGHLIGHTS

★ **ALIANI CASA DEL PARMIGIANO**
A dream for all cheese, sausage and
ham fans ➤ p. 81

★ **SIGNOR BLUM**
3-D wooden puzzles as souvenirs
➤ p. 84

★ **CENEDESE**
Superlative Murano glass ➤ p. 84

**WEST OF
ST MARK'S SQUARE**
Chic fashion,
luxury brands and
breathtaking jewellery

250 m
273 yd

BOOKS

FILIPPI

The city's oldest bookshop as well as a publishing house on Venetian topics: coffee-table books, art, traditional, architecture, everyday life. *Calle del Paradiso 5284 | libreriaeditricefilippi. com | Rialto | stop: Rialto | ▥ K6*

LIBRERIA ACQUA ALTA

Pure chaos and smelling of cat pee. You can't really call this art installation of wheelbarrows full of books and lots of cats everywhere a bookshop. In the courtyard, a special photo location awaits: a tower of books which you can climb.

INSIDER TIP
Take a snap – before it tumbles

WHERE TO START?

Venice's top boutiques are cheek-by-jowl on the **Mercerie**, the narrow rows of shops between St Mark's Square and the Rialto Bridge, as well as along **Calle Larga XXII Marzo** and **Calle Vallaresso**. Bargain-hunters on the hunt for textile and leather goods love browsing through the shops in the alleys to the west of the Rialto Bridge, on the way from there to Campo San Polo and the **Lista di Spagna**, near the railway station, and also **Strada Nova**. The tiny shops in the districts of San Polo and Dorsoduro are full of amusing items, unusual pieces and genuine handmade items.

Owner Luigi has recently handed his shop down to his son, but they have managed to preserve the flair. Visiting is an experience, whether you are going to buy a book or not! *Calle Lunga Santa Maria Formosa 5176 | stop: Ospedale | San Marco | ▥ L6*

LA TOLETTA

This does not refer to the loos, but to a charming bookshop. The name comes from *tole*, i.e. planks of wood that people used in the past to get to a neighbour across a canal. Lots of vintage books. *Sacca della Toletta 1214 | latoletta.com | stop: Accademia | Dorsoduro | ▥ F8*

COSMETICS & SCENTS

SORELLE SFORZA

Let your sense of smell guide you: individual perfumes fruity – tangy or sweet, as you prefer – and room scents made from high-quality natural ingredients. *Calle Seconda dei Saoneri 2658 | stop: San Tomà | Dorsoduro | ▥ F–G6*

SPEZIERIA DE VENEZIA

The luxurious creams and scents are manufactured on Giudecca island – and the scent of flowers, herbs and spices is so strong that you won't want to leave. The Acqua Arabica room scent allows you to take the flair of the Serenissima back home. *Campo San Zaccaria 4695 | spezieriadevenezia. com | stop: San Zaccaria | San Marco | ▥ L7*

The Acqua Alta is a magical bookstore which you won't forget in a hurry

FOOD & DRINK

The foodie hotspot for locals and visitors is around the Mercato di Rialto between the Rialto and Rialto Mercato *vaporetto* stops.

ALIANI CASA DEL PARMIGIANO ★

These people know their cheeses. At Aliani's you get the best Parmesan or exceptional goat's cheese. Everything comes in excellent packaging that preserves the aroma. Don't miss the big favourite: saffron Pecorino. Please note their restricted opening hours: *Mon–Wed 8am–1.30pm, Thu–Sat 8am–7.30pm. Campo Erberia Rialto 214 | alianicasa delparmigiano.it | stop: Rialto Mercato | Rialto | ⅏ J5*

MAURO EL FORNER DE CANTON

Biscotti, bruschette, brigiolini… a great variety of sweet and savoury baked goods. *Ruga Vecchia San Giovanni 603 | elfornerdecanton.com | stop: Rialto Mercato | Rialto | ⅏ H6*

PANTAGRUELICA

Here you can find Ammiana red wine, which is named after a sunken lagoon island and only produced in very small quantities. The grapes are grown on a small island in the lagoon and the wine is highly sought after by collectors! They also sell organic salami, wonderful cheese and much more – all sourced locally from small farmers. *Campo San Barnaba 2844 | stop: Ca' Rezzonico | Dorsoduro | ⅏ E8*

INSIDER TIP
Wine for collectors

RIZZO

This shop sells all those wonderful chocolates and biscuits that you'll want to tuck into straight away, beautifully gift-wrapped for you to take home. Wine, oil, cheese and cold meats are also sold at its five shops, for instance on the *Calle dei Botteri 1719 | rizzovenezia.it | stop: Rialto Mercato | Rialto | ⌐ H5*

VIZIOVIRTÙ

A chocolate boutique selling all sorts of chocolate, including tiny bars, in traditional and exotic flavours. Treat yourself to a cup of Goldoni Hot Chocolate – hot chocolate made without milk or sugar. Heavenly! *Calle Forneri 5988 | viziovirtu.com | stop: Rialto | Rialto | ⌐ K6*

INSIDER TIP
Chocolate heaven

FASHION

ACQUA MAREA

Wellies, wellies and more wellies – a tremendous selection and good prices; colourful boots that will keep your spirits up even during floods! They also sell vegan shoes made of canvas and other natural materials. *Campo San Pantalon 3750 | stop: San Tomà | Dorsoduro | ⌐ E7*

INSIDER TIP
Equipped for acqua alta

BANCO NO. 10

Shopping while doing something for the community at the same time? Of course! Chic and value-for-money dresses, jackets, bags and more made from silk, velvet and brocade by female inmates in the Giudecca prison. All items are unique. *Salizada Sant'Antonin 3478a | stop: San Zaccaria | San Marco | ⌐ M7*

GIULIANA LONGO

Hats in the style of the gondolieri or fancy hats for carnival in this wonderfully old-fashioned hat shop; even trying on the various models is great fun. Every single hat is handmade, and Giuliana will find the right one for any head. *Calle del Lovo 4813 | giulianalongo.com | stop: Rialto | Rialto | ⌐ J6*

MALEFATTE

High-quality organic cosmetics, notepads, t-shirts and original bags made by the inmates of the municipal prison are sold by a cooperative online *(malefatte.org)* and on site, e.g. at the *Bottega Acqua Altra (Campo Santa Margherita 2898 | bottega aquaaltra.tumblr.com | stop: Ca' Rezzonico | Dorsoduro | ⌐ G8)*.

INSIDER TIP
Conscientious shopping

PENNY LANE

This shop will have vintage-lovers gasping for breath. All sort of ordinary and off-the-wall items, organic and FairTrade labels, handbags and accessories made from recycled materials. *Salizada San Pantalon 39 | stop: San Tomà | Dorsoduro | ⌐ E6*

GIFTS & SOUVENIRS

ARRAS

In past centuries, Venice was world

famous for its textile production. Here you find a large selection of colourful, hand-woven silk, woollen and cotton fabrics. *Campiello Squellini 3235 | stop: Ca' Rezzonico | Dorsoduro | ◫ F7*

BASSO

The printer in Venice supplies VIPs all over the world with writing paper and business cards. His printing presses

decorative items. *Campo Santo Stefano 347 | albertovalese-ebru.it | stop: San Samuele, Sant'Angelo | San Marco | ◫ G8*

GILBERTO PENZO

Delightful models of Venetian watercraft. You can also buy do-it-yourself gondola model kits. Gilberto is an expert who knows absolutely

Ideal for luxury shopping or just browsing: the T Fondaco dei Tedeschi

are ancient, and he himself is no spring chicken either. You absolutely must have a look! *Calle del Fumo 5306 | stop: Fondamente Nove | Cannaregio | ◫ L4*

EBRÛ

In the 1980s, Alberto Valese was a pioneer of the marbled paper boom, and he is still considered one of the masters of this guild today. He stocks the full range: handmade paper, book covers and a good selection of

everything about the history and building of gondolas, boats and other ships. *Calle Seconda dei Saoneri 2681 | veniceboats.com | stop: San Tomà | San Polo | ◫ G6*

MADERA

With everything from bedside lamps, tableware, scarves and handbags to unique jewellery, three architects have created a treasure trove of household goods and fashion accessories made of wood, metal and ceramic

Mask-making requires precision

crafted by young designers. *Campo San Barnaba 2762 and Calle Lunga San Barnaba 2729 | maderavenezia.it | stop: Ca' Rezzonico | Dorsoduro | ⊞ E8*

SIGNOR BLUM ★
Three-dimensional, hand-sawn, unmistakably Venetian wooden puzzles – a tasteful present! *Campo San Barnaba 2840 | stop: Ca' Rezzonico | Dorsoduro | ⊞ E8*

T FONDACO DEI TEDESCHI
Luxury apartment store in the old central post office. The ultra-modern architecture in the interior is worth seeing in its own right, and the roof terrace is amazing; but you will

INSIDER TIP
Shopping with a view

need to book a visit online at *dfs.com/en/venice/t-fondaco-rooftop-terrace.* Then there is, of course, the shopping, in particular for luxury brands. *Calle del Fontego dei Tedeschi | stop: Rialto | Rialto | ⊞ J6*

GLASS

CENEDESE ★
For brightly coloured, modern chandeliers. And the plain, slender vases called Vela will go with any interior – they are worth the investment. *Fondamenta Vetrai 68 | simonecenedese.it | stop: Murano | Murano | ⊞ Q4*

GAMBARO & POGGI
For more than a quarter of a century, Mario Gambaro and Bruno Poggi have given full rein to their creativity: vases, jugs, glasses, chandeliers... 1,300 articles in 85 colours that you can admire, and buy, here. *Calle del Cimitero 15 | gambaroepoggiglass.com | stop: Venier | Murano | ⊞ Q2*

PINO SIGNORETTO
The superstar of the glass-blowers. Instead of vases and chandeliers, he creates art in glass. All one-offs, they are eye-wateringly beautiful, but also eye-wateringly expensive. Be sure to visit the showroom – you will be blown away! *Fondamenta Serenella 3 | pinosignoretto.it | stop: Murano | Murano | ⊞ P4*

GLASSES

MICROMEGA
Fantastic eyeglasses crafted in-house

– chic, simple, ultra-light frames made of gold, titanium or horn. *Calle delle Ostreghe 2436 | micromegaottica. com | stop: Giglio | San Marco | ◫ H8*

JEWELLERY

LABERINTHO
Several young goldsmiths have joined forces here to present their imaginative creations. *Calle del Scaleter 2236 | laberintho.it | stop: San Silvestro | San Polo | ◫ G5*

MANUELA ZANVETTORI
This woman knows what women want: necklaces, earrings and bracelets made of glass, gold and silver. She grew up in a family of glass-blowers, so it's understandable that it should be her favourite material. *Fondamenta dei Vetrai 122 | manuelazanvettori. com | stop: Murano | Murano | ◫ Q4*

MASKS

★ *Ca' Macana (Calle de le Botteghe 3172 | camacana.com | stop: Ca' Rezzonico | Dorsoduro | ◫ E8)* have both traditional and super-modern masks – also for children – and all are one-offs. Trying them on is great fun in itself! ★ The master also offers courses in his studio, where you can be initiated into the art of mask-making either in a group or one-on-one. Three other mask producers are much more creative than the mass of suppliers: *Tragicomica (Calle dei Nomboli 2800 | tragicomica.it | stop: San Tomà | San Polo | ◫ G6)*; *Mistero Buffo (Fondamenta San Basilio 1645 |* misterobuffomask.com | stop: San Basilio | Dorsoduro | ◫ D9)*; and *Marega (Fondamenta dell' Osmarin 4968 or 4976a | marega.it | stop: San Zaccaria | San Marco | ◫ L7)*.

SHOES & LEATHER GOODS

BALDUCCI
The softest, smoothest leather from Tuscany, and worked in the Venetian tradition. It started in 1974 with bags, and today it also stocks hand-stitched shoes and belts. *Very classic* and perfect for an elegant occasion. *Rio Terà San Leonardo 1593 | balducciborse. com | stop: Guglie, San Marcuola | San Marco | ◫ F3*

FRATELLI ROSSETTI
A treasure chest for all lovers of fashionable footwear. *Salizada San Moisè 1477 | stop: Vallaresso | San Marco | ◫ J8*

PIEDÀTERRE
The soft-as-silk slippers *(furlane)* with their non-slip rubber soles that the gondolieri wear when they are working used to be available in many shops. Today, cheap reproductions from the Far East have flooded the market. But here you will still find the original – made of linen, with or without silk ribbons in all shades of bright colours. *Ruga degli Oresi 60 | piedaterre-venice.com | stop: Rialto Mercato | Rialto | ◫ J6*

INSIDER TIP
Smart slippers

NIGHTLIFE

Yes, Venice has a nightlife. Unfortunately, it's something that most day-trippers miss – but it's definitely worth experiencing. Some clubs rock until the small hours, and for those who are looking for something really special, La Fenice opera house is the place to go.

Between March and October, you'll be spoilt for choice, with everything from jazz to chamber concerts, and lots in between. And there's plenty of singing and music in churches, monasteries and fraternities all over the city. If you can speak Italian, you will enjoy exploring the world of theatre and cabaret. Some of the productions

Venice's legendary opera house, La Fenice, is a convincing 21st-century reconstruction

are world class; La Fenice in particular is well-known for its lavish performances with all-star casts.

But there are less expensive ways to pass the time: grab a beer or a glass of wine and join the bustling throngs until well after midnight in the *Campi Santa Maria Formosa*, *Santa Margherita*, *Pisani*, *San Barnaba* and *Santi Giovanni e Paolo* – the atmosphere is incomparable. For current information, ask your hotel for the free calendar of events published by the tourist office, or have a look at *unospite divenezia.it, venezianews.it, meetingvenice.it.*

WHERE TO GO OUT IN VENICE

🚆 Venezia
Santa Lucia

Gallion

Canal Grande

Salizada San Stae

Calle Longa

Calle dei Boteri

Fondamenta Rio Marin

Corte Canal

Calle de la Laca

Campo
San Polo

Rio Terà

CAMPO SANTA MARGHERITA
Vivid nightlife in front of Gothic palazzi

Crosera

Calle Contarini

Campo
Santa
Margherita

Calle Bernardo

📍 Venice Jazz Club ★

Fondamenta Girardini

Calle Lunga de San Barnaba

🏛 Ca'Rezzonico

Teatro La Fenice ★ 📍

Campo
Santo
Stefano

📍 Interpreti Veneziani ★

ZATTERE
Bustling gastro scene with a view of Giudecca

Fondamenta Nani

Rio Terà Antonio Foscarini

Piscina Venier

Canal Grande

Fondamenta de Ca' Balà

Fondamenta Zattere al Ponte Longo

Fondamenta Zattere ai Gesuati

🏛 Zattere

Canale della Giudecca

▲ N
200 m
219 yd

RIVA DEGLI SCHIAVONI

Enjoy a sundowner on this elegant waterfront promenade

Fondamente Nove

Calle del Fumo

Calle Verdi

Fondamente Nove

Calle de la Testa

Barbaria de le Tole

Salizada San Lio

Ruga Giuffa

Calle dei Fabbri

Calle Frezzaria

Piazza San Marco

Molo di Palazzo Ducale

Riva degli Schiavoni

S. Zaccaria

San Marco

Bacino di S. Marco

MARCO POLO HIGHLIGHTS

★ **VENICE JAZZ CLUB**
Jam sessions in a relaxed atmosphere ➤ p. 92

★ **INTERPRETI VENEZIANI**
Baroque music by Bach, Vivaldi & co. in the former church of San Vidal ➤ p. 93

★ **TEATRO LA FENICE**
Opera, dance and concerts in the city's oldest theatre ➤ p.95

BARS, PUBS, CLUBS, CAFÉS & LIVE MUSIC

ART BLU CAFFÈ

A bright and friendly eatery with a functional modern look. Tip: the terrace with its amazing panorama is ideal for a nightcap at the end of the day. *Daily until 11pm | Campo Santo Stefano 2808a | stop: San Samuele | San Marco | ⌂ G8*

BACARO JAZZ

Cocktails and tapas bar (until 2am) with a unique and colourful ambience. An ideal place for jazz lovers and night owls. *Daily 11am–approx. 2.30am, happy hour 4–6pm | Salizada del Fondaco dei Tedeschi 5546 | stop: Rialto | Rialto | ⌂ J6*

B-BAR

Fancy some celebrity-watching? The VIP presence in the lounge of the luxury Hotel Bauer is traditionally high.

WHERE TO START?

The liveliest places are **Campo Santa Margherita**, **Campo San Pantalon** and along the wide **canals of Cannaregio**. There are rows and rows of bars, pubs and artists' cafés, some with live performances. The Venetians also like to meet up in **Campo San Bartolomeo** or **Campo San Lio**. On hot summer nights you can enjoy the ⚑ **open-air establishments on the Canal Grande** next to the Fabbriche Vecchie.

So order yourself a cocktail (they really are extremely good!) and relax in an armchair. Musicians and Hollywood stars – the likes of Sting, Al Pacino or Daniel Craig often pop in for a drink. *In winter Fri/Sat 7pm–midnight (with live music 9 euros), in summer Bar Canale on the terrace of the Hotel Bauer daily 7pm–midnight | Campo San Moisè 1459 | bbarvenezia.com | stop: Vallaresso | San Marco | ⌂ J8*

CAFÉ NOIR

Quirky but charming bar with a stylish interior and unusually reasonable prices. Popular among students and the happy hour *aperitivi* are very good value. *Mon–Sat 7am–2am, Sun 9am–2am | Crosera San Pantalon 3805 | stop: San Tomà | Dorsoduro | ⌂ E–F7*

CAFFÈ ROSSO

In a lovely spot that is bustling until well after midnight. An absolute hotspot of the open-air nightlife, with live music in summer and – comparatively – low prices. Be sure to try the delicious *tramezzini*! *Mon–Sat 7am–1am | Campo Santa Margherita 2963 | stop: Ca' Rezzonico | Dorsoduro | ⌂ E7*

CANTINA VECIA CARBONERA

During the day, this bar serves the best *cicchetti*, and in the evening it is one of the buzziest spots, with live music twice a week. A young audience, relaxed atmosphere and good barkeepers. Easy to find on the corner of the main Strada Nova. *Closed Mon | Ponte Sant'Antonio 2329 | stop: San Marcuola | Cannaregio | ⌂ H3*

If you're in need of sustenance, head for the Cantina Vecia Carbonera

CENTRALE

Trendy restaurant-bar with international flair. The food is well above average and the atmosphere stylish, but it is pricey. *7pm–1am, Fri/Sat until 2am | Piscina Frezzeria 1659 | caffe centralevenezia.com | stop: Vallaresso | San Marco | ⫘ J8*

CHET BAR

This small pub with a great menu and good music fills up later in the evening – very popular with young local people and students. The clientele tends towards the alternative rather than the well-heeled. You get a glass of wine for only 2 euros and cocktails from 5–8 euros. Opening hours vary depending on the day and numbers of patrons, but they are always open until late.

INSIDER TIP
Lots of fun for little money

Campo Santa Margherita 3684 | stop: Ca' Rezzonico | Dorsoduro | ⫘ E7

CORNER PUB

What once attracted lovers of British beer and sandwiches, now also offers Venetian rolls and *cicchetti*, ensuring a varied clientele. Apart from local people, you now find many students from the UK who are looking for a touch of home. *Wed–Mon 10.30am–1am | Calle della Chiesa 684 | stop: Accademia | Dorsoduro | ⫘ G9*

IL SANTO BEVITORE

Twenty types of high-quality draught beer for those who are getting a little tired of wine and spritzes. Always a pleasant atmosphere. *Daily from 4pm–2am | Campo Santa Fosca 2393a | ilsantobevitorepub.com | stop: San Marcuola | Cannaregio | ⫘ H3*

MARGARET DUCHAMP

"In" bar with lovely barkeepers. The cocktails are among the best in the city, and the Campo is active until late at night. Open until 2am. *Closed Tue | Campo Santa Margherita 3019 | stop: Ca' Rezzonico | San Dorsoduro | ⌑ E7*

TARNOWSKA'S AMERICAN BAR

A stylish place to enjoy yourself, and not just for the guests of the adjoining hotel. Good cocktails, comfortable club chairs: James Bond would be a regular. Named after a Russian countess who had one of her many lovers murdered in the Palazzo Maurogonato which is now the Ala Hotel. If that's not reason enough to have a vodka... Here you can also sometimes enjoy live music Frank Sinatra style. Barkeeper Rey is an institution and will mix your favourite drink. *Campo Santa Maria del Giglio | stop: Giglio | San Marco | ⌑ H8*

UN MONDO DI VINO

Tiny pub with delicious *cicchetti* and not much room. A glass of wine costs between 1.50 and 3 euros. The later the hour, the longer the queue outside the door. *Daily from 10am–11.30pm | Salizada San Canciano 5984 | FB: UnMondoDivinoVenice | stop: Ca' d'Or | Cannaregio | ⌑ K5*

VENICE JAZZ CLUB ★

A bit like a living room party. Guests sit together with finger food and relaxed

The Campo Santa Margherita is always full of life

music, then there's some jazz (the in-house band is the VJC Quartet), and by the end of the evening they're all the best of friends. *Happy hour from 7pm, concert starts at 9pm Mon–Wed, Fri, Sat 7pm–1am | Ponte dei Pugni 3102 | venicejazzclub.com | stop: Ca' Rezzonico | Dorsoduro | ⬛ E8*

CASINO

☂ Today, you can try your luck behind the impressive façade of the *Palazzo Vendramin-Calergi* on the Canal Grande. Roulette, blackjack, gaming machines, etc. *Daily 3.30pm–2.45am; in summer 4pm–2.45am | casino venezia.it | stop: San Marcuola | Cannaregio | ⬛ G4*

CINEMA

Most of the films shown in the few remaining cinemas in Venice have been dubbed into Italian but there is one exception:

CASA DEL CINEMA

This meeting place for cineastes shows high-quality films from all over the world, often in the original language with Italian subtitles. *Salizada San Stae 1990 | tel. 04 15 24 13 20 | stop: San Stae | San Polo | ⬛ G5*

CONCERTS

COLLEGIUM DUCALE

The chamber orchestra, founded in 1993, performs wonderful instrumental works from the Baroque and Romantic periods. Opera singers also perform the favourite arias from *Carmen*, *Othello* and other operas accompanied by a piano. The venues are just as impressive: the *Palazzo delle Prigioni (⬛ L8)* and the "Blue Room" of the *Teatro San Gallo (⬛ J7)*. *Tel. 0 41 98 81 55 | collegiumducale. com*

INTERPRETI VENEZIANI ★

This chamber music group gives concerts entitled "Violins in Venice" on more than 200 days of the year in the former church of San Vidal. The highlights of the programme include works by Bach, Vivaldi and other classical composers. *Tel. 04 12 77 05 61 | interpretiveneziani.com | stop: Accademia | San Marco | ⬛ G8*

SCUOLA GRANDE DI SAN GIOVANNI EVANGELISTA

This, the oldest brotherhood in Venice, dates from 1261 and is an incredible location, providing a stunning combination of Gothic architecture and Venetian Baroque with lots of stucco. It's highly atmospheric and they programme a colourful mixture of exhibitions and music events. Performances are given at irregular intervals, which is why you should check their schedule in advance. *Campiello della Scuola 2454 | scuola sangiovanni.it | stop: Ferrovia | Cannaregio | ⬛ F5–6*

VIRTUOSI DI VENEZIA

Baroque orchestral music hits, ranging from Vivaldi's *Four Seasons* to Albinoni's *Adagio* – as well as arias by Mozart, Verdi and Donizetti. Dressed in period costume, the Virtuosi di Venezia give several concerts of opera and orchestral classics weekly in the *Ateneo di San Basso* behind St Mark's Basilica. *Piazzetta dei Leoni | tel. 04 15 28 28 25 | virtuosidivenezia. com | stop: Vallaresso | San Marco | ⌑ K7*

PARTY VENUES

In summer, people head to the Lido to party. Travel out on the night *vaporetto* (line N) from San Zaccaria. Disembark and head straight for the beach. In the evenings, the bathing spots become lounge bars with DJ sets, such as the *Pachuka (daily from 9am–10pm, later at weekends Viale Klinger/Spiaggia San Nicolò)*. The *Beach Terrace (Lungomare Guglielmo Marconi 22)* is a fish restaurant, pizzeria and cocktail bar rolled into one. Or do like the young Venetians

INSIDER TIP
Night-time snack on the beach

do, and stock up on snacks and drinks at one of the beach kiosks, then find yourself a pleasant spot – for instance at the *Chiosco Bahiano* on the northern end of the beach on the *Piazza Pola*.

There are no big discos in the city centre; there simply isn't the space, and noise pollution is also an issue. But on the plus side, at the *Piccolo Mondo (⌑ F9) (daily 11pm–4am | Calle Contarini Corfù 1056a | Dorsoduro | stop: Accademia)* you can dance until 4am. Lots of international artists tend to pop in late at night, as well as Venetians. Even Mick Jagger

has been spotted here… The cheapest parties in town take place in the open air at

INSIDER TIP
Party in front of the palazzo

🐖 *Campo Santa Margeherita* and *Campo San Bartolomeo*, with their historic palazzi as the backdrop. Join the locals, and bring-your-own food and drink.

SHOWS

VENEZIA – THE SHOW
An elaborate multimedia spectacle: actors in historical costumes talk (simultaneous English translation through headphones) about Venice's more than 1,000 years of history supported by cutting-edge digital technology. The show can also be booked together with a buffet dinner. *Campo San Gallo 1097 | tel. 04 12 41 20 02 | teatrosangallo.net | stop: Vallaresso | San Marco | ⌑ J7*

VENICE MUSIC PROJECT
A kind of high-end travelling musical circus, performing both sacred and secular music (e.g. the ancient repertoire of the gondolieri), instrumentally or accompanied by singers, at a variety of atmospheric venues. Browse their events schedule to see what interests you. The programme also includes lesser known composers. *Tel. 34 57 91 19 48 | venicemusicproject.it*

THEATRE & OPERA

MUSICA IN MASCHERA
Opera lovers may want to skip this chapter, because what the opera and

ballet evenings in the *Scuola Grande dei Carmini* have to offer, cannot always be called great art. However, this music and dance ensemble performs in original 18th-century costumes and will take you back to an era when such evening entertainment was for Venetians what television is for us today: a pleasant way to relax. *Calle de la Pazienza/Calle de la Scuola | musicainmaschera.it | stop: Ca' Rezzonico | Dorsoduro | ⚏ D–E 7–8*

TEATRO GOLDONI

Wonderful slapstick – from the past! The comedies, which playwright Carlo Goldoni brought to the stage in the 18th century, are as charming as ever. His "Arlecchino Furioso" character will never go out of fashion. Make sure you get tickets as near to the front as possible so that you can read the English subtitles. In the break, you can enjoy a free Bellini in the courtyard. *Calle del Teatro 4650 | tel. 04 12 40 20 14 | teatrostabileveneto.it | stop: Rialto | Rialto | ⚏ J6–7*

INSIDER TIP
Theatre with subtitles

TEATRO LA FENICE ★

The theatre burned to the ground in 1996, but the old "Phoenix" rose again from the ashes and was reopened in 2003 – *dov'era e com'era* (where and as it was) – on Campo Fantin in the form of a time-honoured, golden shimmering theatre with rows of boxes. In Venice, tickets for the excellently cast opera and dance performances (the Fenice is one of Europe's leading opera houses), as

Teatro Maliban, a temple to the muses

well as concerts, are available from the theatre's box office and the Ve.La. ticket offices at the railway station and Piazzale Roma. Information and tickets from abroad: tel. 0 41 24 24. *Campo San Fantin 1965 | teatrola fenice.it | stop: Giglio | San Marco | ⚏ H8*

TEATRO MALIBRAN

Opera, ballet, concerts and plays since 1678; some in cooperation with the Teatro Fenice. *Campiello del Teatro 5864 | tel. 0 41 24 24 | teatrolafenice. it | stop: Rialto | Rialto | ⚏ K5–6*

ACTIVE & RELAXED

Punta della Dogana – a lovely spot for contemplating the sea

SPORT & WELLNESS

CRUISE THE CANALS

Exploring the labyrinth of canals on your own is an adventure. Instead of being driven, you become your own captain. A recommended rental firm for both rowing boats and motorised watercraft is *Giampietro Brussa (Fondamenta Labia 331 | tel. 0 41 71 57 87 | brussaisboat.it | stop: Guglie ☐ F3)* near the Ponte delle Guglie.

EXPLORE THE ISLANDS BY BIKE

A few hours of cycling along the seashore can be a wonderful alternative to the many hours spent wandering the city. On Sant'Erasmo, for example, you'll have fields and gardens on one side, and salt marshes and sandbanks on the other. The round trip of the island is 10km, and the going is manageable for most people. Bicycles are for hire at *Il Lato Azzurro* hotel and restaurant *(Via dei Forti 13 | tel. 04 15 23 06 42 | latoazzurro.it).*

The Lido is ideal for longer tours. Bicycles can be rented at the Lido *vaporetto* stop: *Gardin (tel. 04 12 76 00 05 | biciclettegardin.com)* on Piazzale Santa Maria Elisabetta 2 or *Renato Scarpi (tel. 04 15 26 80 19 | lidoonbike.it)* at Viale Santa Maria Elisabetta 21b. From there, you can pedal off towards the south as far as the picturesque villages of Malamocco and Alberoni and, if you have the time and the fitness, ride past Pellestrina to the small fishing town of Chioggia.

ROWING ALLA VENEZIANA

Why not learn to do what the gondolieri do? Two traditional rowing clubs, *Reale Società Canottieri Bucintoro (Fondamenta Zattere 263 | tel. 04 15 20 56 30 | bucintoro.org | stop: Spirito Santo | individual sessions 3–5 hrs 100 euros, group sessions 85 euros/person | ☐ H10)* and *Reale Società Canottieri Francesco Querini*

The Lido is perfect for cycling trips, although you won't need a mountain bike

(Fondamente Nove 6576e | tel. 04 15 22 20 39 | canottieriquerini.it | stop: Ospedale | 8 sessions of 1½ hrs 130 euros, individual sessions of 1½ hrs 80 euros | ⏍ M5) give short courses where even beginners and children can learn how to steer a *sandolo*, a *mascareta* or a *gondola* elegantly over the water and through the canals.

JOGGING & BATHING AT THE LIDO

If you need a break from the narrow, stone streets of the historic centre, cross over to the Lido. The long, sandy beach is perfect for jogging. The narrow, 12-km-long island, which shields Venice and the lagoon from the open sea, became fashionable for bathing towards the end of the 19th century, and cinema fans will know this from Luchino Visconti's cinematic adaptation of Thomas Mann's *Death in Venice*. Today, the atmosphere is much more relaxed, except for the period

when movie stars from all over the world hold court in the Palazzo del Cinema during the Venice Film Festival. In summer, jumping into the waves is a wonderful way to cool off, but don't swim in the canals: there are hefty fines for doing so!

WELLNESS WITH A VIEW

Why not indulge in a spa treatment *and* enjoy the panoramic views of the Giudecca canal and St Mark's Square? You can do both at the *Palladio Hotel & Spa (Fondamenta Zitelle 33 | tel. 04 15 20 70 22 | palladiohotelspa.com | stop: Zitelle | ⏍ K11)*, a luxurious five-star establishment within the walls of an ancient monastery. The gardens are beautiful too and, when sunny, you can have a massage among the trees and flowers. This former home for unmarried young women without a dowry, known as *zitelle*, is just the place for a girls' weekend away!

FESTIVALS & EVENTS

JANUARY

Festa della Befana (6 January): On Sant'Erasmo, a fire is lit and children are given presents by the good witch (*befana*).

FEBRUARY/MARCH

★ **Venice Carnival** This legendary festivity, with hundreds of events, balls and an ocean of masks all over the city, starts with the *Volo dell' Angelo*, the "Flight of the Angel", at which a young woman dressed in historic costume floats above St Mark's Square. *carnevale.venezia.it* (for details).

MARCH/APRIL

Su e Zo per i Ponti (last Sunday in March or first Sunday in April): Fun run "up and down the bridges". *suezo.it*

Benedizione del Fuoco (Maundy Thursday): When St Mark's Basilica glows in the light of thousands of candles.

Yachting in Venice Boat exhibition at a weekend in the middle of April, with yachts to look at and board, and a programme for children.

Festa di San Marco (25 April): With a solemn Mass in the Basilica, gondola races on the Canal Grande and festivities on the Piazza.

MAY/JUNE

Vogalonga (the Sunday at the end of May/beginning of June): More than 5,000 amateur rowers fight it out on a 30-km-long route from Bacino San Marco to Burano and back via Murano. The regatta is open to all, as long as you have your own boat and sufficient staying power. Information and booking: *tel. 04 15 21 05 44 | vogalonga. com*

Festa della Sensa (Sunday after Ascension): "Marriage of the Sea" with a historical fleet sailing from San Marco to the Lido.

Wearing a mask is one of the rules of the Carnival

MID MAY-EARLY NOVEMBER
★ **Art Biennale** In uneven years at the former shipyard Arsenale in the east of the district of Castello, and spread all over the city. Exhibitions, private views and events, all based on contemporary art: paintings, sculptures, installations, dance and theatre. The exhibition pavilions are also architecturally interesting. *labiennale.org*

JUNE
Salone Nautico International boat show in the Arsenale area. *salone nautico.venezia.it*

JULY
Redentore (third Sunday in July): "Feast of the Saviour" – a procession to the Redentore church and an amazing fireworks display the night before.

SEPTEMBER
Regata Storica (first weekend in September): Thousands of festively decorated boats with costumed crews glide down the Canal Grande.
International Film Festival Eleven days of film on the Lido. *labiennale.org*
Fish Festival (third Sunday in September): With vast quantities of *pesce fritto*, deep-fried fish.

OCTOBER
⚑ **Wine Festival** (first or second Sunday in October): on Sant'Erasmo with music, dancing, feasting and a regatta.
Venice Marathon (late October): Starting in the town of Stra. *venicemarathon.it*

NOVEMBER
Madonna della Salute (21 November): Procession over pontoons to the church followed by a feast with raisin donuts and wine.

SLEEP WELL

BOAT & BREAKFAST

What an experience, to have breakfast on board and watch the sunset on deck! While the cabins of the *Sarah Sun Cruise (Canale dei Lavraneri | tel. 34 66 51 41 29 | stop: Sacca Fisola | sarahcruisevenezia.it | € | Sacca Fisola | ⊞ C10)* are small, they come fully equipped. The yacht is moored opposite the Hilton Hotel on Sacca Fisola.

CHEAP BUT STYLISH

A 19th-century grain store on Giudecca island has been transformed into hip accommodation with a quirky mix of styles: the *Generator Hostel (27 rooms with 235 beds | Fondamenta Zitelle 86 | tel. 04 18 77 82 88 | generatorhostels.com | stop: Zitelle | € | Giudecca | ⊞ J11)* is full of backpackers from around the world. You get a bed in the dormitory from 16 euros and a double room with bath for 60 euros.

FEASTING & SLEEPING

The *Venissa (Fondamenta Santa Caterina 3 | tel. 04 15 27 22 81 | venissa.it | stop: Mazzorbo | €€ | Mazzorbo | ⊞ V1)* on the small island of Mazzorbo has an adjoining Michelin-starred organic restaurant. The vegetables are home-grown, as is most of the wine; after your feast you will sleep comfortably in one of the six bedrooms in country-house style.

INSIDER TIP
Connoisseur tip

IN THE GHETTO

Stay in the heart of the former Jewish Ghetto, away from the crowds, in a 600-year-old building one floor below the former synagogue. The *Locanda del Ghetto* is well looked after, provides a good kosher breakfast and pleasant service. The two junior suites have terraces overlooking the square. *6 rooms | Campo del Ghetto Novo 2892 | tel.*

The Palazzina G, styled by Philippe Starck, is great for spotting celebrities

04 12 75 92 92 | locandadelghetto. net | stop: Guglie | €€ | Ghetto | ⚏ F2.

LUXURY WITH STYLE

Are you paying a lot of money for stuffy old-fashioned grandeur? Not here. Designer Philippe Starck has turned this small building next to the museum Palazzo Grassi into a contemporary five-star boutique hotel. With much attention to detail, the lobby, lounge and restaurant/bar have been outfitted with a mix of vintage furniture and lush colours, while the 26 rooms have been kept all in white. The *Palazzina G (Ramo Grassi 3247 | tel. 04 15 28 46 44 | palazzinagrassi. com | stop: San Samuele | €€€ | San Marco | ⚏ F7–8)* is favoured by the stars. On Saturday nights DJs will entertain you until the early morning.

NO PRAYERS THESE DAYS

Once an abbey guesthouse, now privately run. Still spartan, but bright, clean and inexpensive, and with friendly hosts. The fabulous location of the *Domus Ciliota (50 rooms | Calle delle Muneghe 2976 | tel. 04 15 20 48 88 | ciliota.it | stop: San Samuele | € | San Marco | ⚏ G8)* near the Campo Santo Stefano means you don't need so many *vaporetto* rides.

OFF THE BEATEN TRACK

In the lagoon village of Malamocco in the outermost corner of the Lido you can meet fishermen and farmers and learn to cook from the delightful hostesses Michela and Micaela in the *Relais Alberti (Campo della Chiesa 3 | tel. 04 15 26 11 43 | stop: Lido, bus A/B to Malamocco | relaisalberti.com | €€ | Lido-Malamocco | ⚏ 0).* The hotel is decorated with antique furniture and beautiful soft furnishings. They also rent out bicycles and organise boat trips on the lagoon.

DISCOVERY TOURS

Do you want to get under the skin of the city? Then these discovery tours provide the perfect guide. They include advice on which sights to visit, tips on where to stop for that perfect holiday snap, a choice of the best places to eat and drink and suggestions for fun activities.

Looking across the Canal Grande to the Pescheria

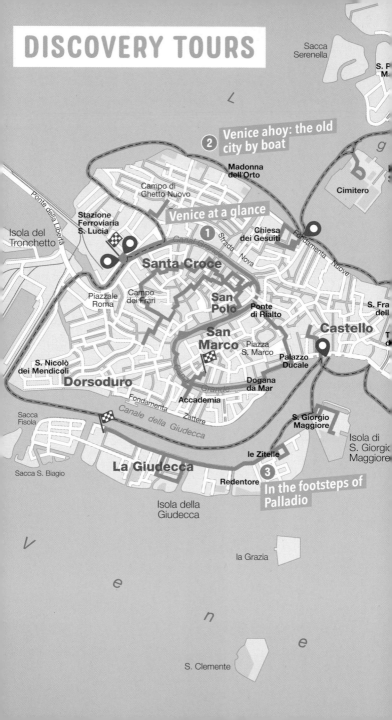

DISCOVERY TOURS

② Venice ahoy: the old city by boat

① Venice at a glance

③ In the footsteps of Palladio

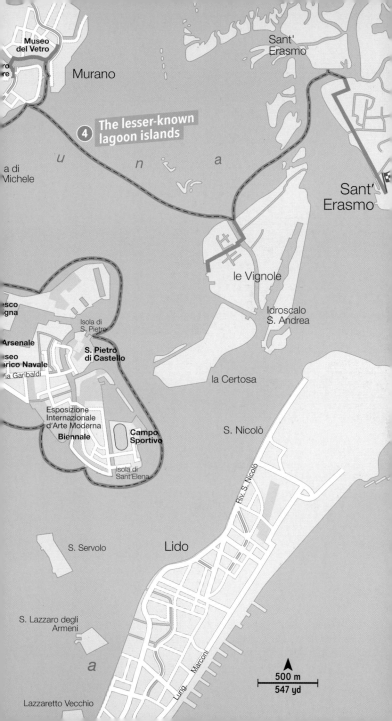

Museo
del Vetro

Murano

Sant'
Erasmo

a di
Michele

④ The lesser-known
lagoon islands

u   n   i   a

Sant'
Erasmo

le Vignole

Idroscalo
S. Andrea

esco
gna

Isola di
S. Pietro

Arsenale

S. Pietro
di Castello

seo
rico Navale

ia Garibaldi

la Certosa

S. Nicolò

Esposizione
Internazionale
d'Arte Moderna

Biennale

Campo
Sportivo

Isola di
Sant'Elena

S. Servolo

Lido

Riv. S. Nicolò

S. Lazzaro degli
Armeni

a

500 m
547 yd

Lazzaretto Vecchio

Lung

Marconi

❶ VENICE AT A GLANCE

➤ The best of Venice in just one eventful day
➤ Rialto market, Frari church, St Mark's Square and more
➤ Market in the morning and music in the evening

📍 Santa Lucia railway station

🏁 Art Blu Caffè

→ approx. 12km

🚶 1 day (about 3½ hrs total walking time)

You can vary the starting point of this tour depending on the location of your hotel - just start from the closest *vaporetto* stop to your neighbourhood.

ℹ️ You can only tour the **Cathedral** and climb the **Campanile** at the suggested times during the peak season (Easter–October). At other times of the year these attractions close earlier. You should try to purchase concert tickets well in advance of your trip.

---

❶ Santa Lucia railway station

❷ Caffè del Doge

❸ Pescheria

From ❶ Santa Lucia railway station, *take a Line 1 vaporetto to San Silvestro.* In the morning light, the glistening façades of the palaces along the Canal Grande breeze past – there really is no better way to begin a day exploring the grandeur of this city on a lagoon. Stop for a cappuccino and a croissant at ❷ Caffè del Doge ➤ p.70, *then head northwest to the* ❸ Pescheria ➤ p.33. Stroll past the fishmongers' stalls *(Tue–Sat)* and enjoy this amazing feast for the eyes even if you don't plan on buying anything!

COFFEE IN THE MIDST OF VENETIAN DAILY LIFE

❹ Campo Santa Margherita

Continue walking from the market through the alleys to the ❹ Campo Santa Margherita ➤ p.54, *which is just a ten-minute walk away.* Go past Campo San Polo and the Frari Church and then sit down at one of the tables at Caffè Rosso ➤ p.90 *on the western side of the square.* It's a great place to observe the goings-on of daily life in Venice, away from the tourist crowds.

After a short break, *make your way back to the* ❺ Frari Church ➤ p.52. It's worth it just to see Titian's pyramid-shaped tomb and the picture of Christ's Ascension above the main altar. *Right next door* is the ❻ Scuola Grande di San Rocco ➤ p.52. Make sure to take a good look at the main hall which is adorned with 56 paintings by Jacopo Tintoretto.

INSIDER TIP
A feast of the arts

❺ **Frari Church**

❻ **Scuola Grande di San Rocco**

VENICE'S MOST UNUSUAL ICE CREAM

Afterwards, walk through the *alleyways of San Polo* with its souvenir and crafts shops. *Take a little detour to Santa Croce* and check out Carlo Pistacchi's *gelateria* ❼ Alaska ➤ p.70, which sells quirky ice-cream flavours such as asparagus or artichoke. Carlo's specialities – often produced as sorbets, i.e. without milk or cream, and without any added sugar – have little in common with conventional ice cream, but their flavours are unique. Your next destination is one of the most impressive *palaces on the Canal Grande,* which now houses the ❽ Galleria d'Arte Moderna ➤ p.32. The collection in Ca' Pesaro contains a representative selection of 19th- and 20th-century art.

❼ **Alaska**

❽ **Galleria d'Arte Moderna**

❾ **Do Mori**

❿ **Piazza San Marco**

A number of quaint, old wine taverns *around the Rialto Bridge* have survived the various waves of modernisation intact. The oldest of these so-called *bacari* is the picture-perfect ❾ Do Mori ➤ p.68. No longer an insider tip and therefore always packed, it belongs to Venice just like St Mark's Basilica. An absolute must-see! Enjoy fabulous wine and delicious *cicchetti* at the bar!

The vaporetto line 1 (Rialto Mercato stop) will take you straight to the ❿ Piazza San Marco ➤ p.35 in a few minutes. Visit St Mark's Basilica, enjoy the fabulous views from the Campanile. Then watch the masses

Venice's oldest *bacaro,* Do Mori

on St Mark's Square from the ⑪ American Bar ➤ p. 66, a standing bar *at the foot of the clock tower.*

WHAT ABOUT SOME RETAIL THERAPY?

Fancy a bit of shopping? *Then stroll through the* ⑫ Mercerie *towards the Rialto Bridge.* Almost all major fashion designers have boutiques along the narrow streets, which are also dotted with enticing shops selling exquisite jewellery and antiques. *At the Rialto stop, hop aboard a line 1 vaporetto and get off at Accademia.*

⑫ Mercerie

NOW FOR A GLASS OF WINE

Follow along the eastern flank of the famous gallery of paintings until you come to the Hotel Ca' Pisani. You might be tempted to stay longer than you originally planned in its basement wine bar ⑬ La Rivista ➤ p. 68, which serves snacks, cheese platters and wines by the glass.

⑬ La Rivista

However, you don't really want to let your tickets for a concert at the ⑭ Interpreti Veneziani ➤ p. 93 go to waste. Experience Baroque chamber music at its finest surrounded by the atmospheric ambiance of a former church: *cross the Ponte dell'Accademia to get to San Vidal in less than five minutes.*

⑭ Interpreti Veneziani

ARE YOU STILL HUNGRY?

Time for some food now? *Close by*, the ⑮ Art Blu Caffè ➤ p. 90 serves large and small snacks and good drinks, along with fabulous views of the Campo Santo Stefano by night! Many of the customers here are students; it is easy to get talking and soon it's after midnight – an ideal end to a relaxed evening.

⑮ Art Blu Caffè

❷ VENICE AHOY: THE OLD CITY BY BOAT

➤ Boat trip including sightseeing
➤ Island hopping on a *vaporetto*
➤ Off the beaten track: Cannaregio, Ghetto, San Michele, Murano

📍	Santa Lucia railway station	🏁	Santa Lucia railway station
↻	approx. 25km	⛴	1 day (2 hrs total travelling time)
ℹ	Lines 4.1 and 4.2 run every 20 mins during the day.		

The starting point for this tour is the ❶ Santa Lucia railway station. *Outside the station, at the bottom of*

❶ Santa Lucia railway station

Artisan glassblower on Murano

the steps, board one of the floating buses called a vaporetto, so characteristic of the city of canals, serving line 4.2 (line 4.1 travels the same route, but in the opposite direction). At first, the boat chugs briefly along the Canal Grande, but immediately after passing the impressive church of San Geremia, it turns left onto the Canale di Cannaregio.

AN INSIGHT INTO VENICE'S JEWISH PAST

Leaving the Palazzo Labia behind, the route continues into the unusually spacious and bright district – at least by Venetian standards – of Cannaregio. *You should interrupt your journey at the first stop (Ponte delle Guglie)* and walk to the former Jewish ❷ Ghetto ➤ p. 47, the oldest in the world, which has a fabulous museum. If you're thirsty, pop into the Jewish restaurant ❸ Ghimel Garden ➤ p. 75 – it's worth it just to see the garden.

❷ Ghetto

❸ Ghimel Garden

Back on the vaporetto, pass under the triple arches of the Ponte dei Tre Archi and out into the open water. The views reach as far as the islands of Burano and Torcello, and to the airport. The boat speeds up and heads east. *Stay on as far as Fondamente Nove,* then stretch your legs on land for a few minutes. How about a look at the Jesuit church of ❹ Santa Maria Assunta dei Gesuiti ➤ p. 49? It's an impressive and imposing example of Baroque architecture. ❺ Titian's house is somewhat less overpowering.

❹ Santa Maria Assunta dei Gesuiti

❺ Titian's house

AN ENTIRE ISLAND FOR A CEMETERY

By no means should you miss out on *a walk across the cemetery island of* ❻ San Michele ➤ p. 61, with its quite special atmosphere and famous graves, such as those of Igor Stravinsky and Sergei Diaghilev. *The northernmost point along this round-trip route* is the island of ❼ Murano ➤ p. 61, famous for its traditional glass-blowing industry. Art lovers should definitely take a look inside the churches of San Pietro Martire and Santi Maria e Donato. Souvenir shoppers, on the other hand, should make their way to one of the glassblowers' workshops that is open to visitors.

❻ San Michele

❼ Murano

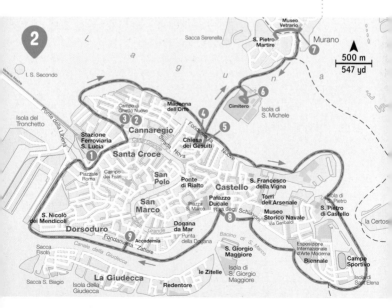

Return to the Fondamente Nove stop and take the vaporetto along the northern shore of the Castello district. It passes the Franciscan church called San Francesco della Vigna and navigates around the San Pietro di Castello and Isola di Sant'Elena peninsulas. Once it reaches the San Marco basin, it steers past the Biennale exhibition grounds to the west. As you pass by ⑧ **Riva degli Schiavoni**

⑧ Riva degli Schiavoni

, the wide quay that is a popular place for a stroll, you can enjoy the parade of some of the most famous hotels in the city.

ENJOY AN ICE CREAM & WATCH THE BOATS GO BY
Get off the boat one last time at San Zaccaria, buy yourself a super-creamy ice cream at ⑨ **Gelateria Nico**

⑨ Gelateria Nico

(Fondamenta Zattere al Ponte Longo 922 | gelaterianico. com) – their speciality being *gianduiotto*, nougat ice cream with real cream – and take a stroll along this famous promenade. Here you can watch the activities on the water: barges, yachts, fishing boats and, in between, the gondolas that bounce around like black dots on the waves. *Once you are back on the boat,* you will drift past the island of Giudecca before coming to the *ferry harbour and crossing under the controversial* Ponte della Costituzione ➤ p. 31 *to return to* ① Santa Lucia railway station.

① Santa Lucia railway station

❸ IN THE FOOTSTEPS OF PALLADIO

➤ Monasteries, towers and churches
➤ Breathtaking Renaissance architecture
➤ Finish with a drink at the rooftop bar

📍	San Marco-San Zaccaria vaporetto stop	🏁 Skyline Rooftop Bar
→	approx. 3km on foot	🚶 3–4 hrs (about 45 mins total walking time)

Take a line 2 vaporetto from the ❶ San Marco-San Zaccaria stop to cross over to San Giorgio Maggiore in a matter of minutes. As you do so, you can capture the most popular photo motif on the lagoon, namely the monastery of ❷ San Giorgio Maggiore. It was built for the Benedictines at the end of the 16th century by Andrea Palladio, the most famous architect of his time, on the picturesque island across from the Doge's Palace.

❶ San Marco-
San Zaccaria stop

❷ San Giorgio
Maggiore

A HIGHLIGHT:
THE VIEWS FROM THE CAMPANILE
Once you have reached the church itself, take a moment to fully appreciate the geometrical austerity of its dazzling white marble façade, reminiscent of an ancient temple, before you take a look at the equally impressive interior of this three-nave church with its large Tintoretto paintings. The panoramic view from the top of the Campanile di San Giorgio Maggiore (daily 9.30am–12.30pm and 2.30–6pm, in winter until 4.30pm) is just as breathtaking as the view from the Campanile of San Marco across the way, but there are fewer tourists around.

SECRET GARDENS
From San Giorgio, cross to the long island of Giudecca – just one stop further on the same line. The stop at Zitelle

Andrea Palladio's masterpiece, San Giorgio Maggiore, is a Venetian landmark

gets its name from the convent for unmarried girls *(zitelle)* that Palladio built here. The convent's church is Santa Maria della Presentazione. Stroll around the church to discover four wonderful gardens brought back to life by Francesca Bortolotto Possati, the owner of the marvellous Palladio Hotel & Spa, which can today be found inside the convent's walls.

INSIDER TIP
First pray, then weed

Stroll along the beach as far as Palladio's magnificent church of ❹ Il Redentore *(Mon 10.30am–4pm, Tue–Sat 10.30am–4.30pm)* with its Classical dome and brilliant marble façade. It was built in the late 16th century as a plea to God to end the plague, which was devastating the city at that time. Every year the Redentore, "Feast of the Saviour", which commemorates the end of the epidemic, takes place here on the third Sunday in July.

A VISIT TO A 1920S FASHION ICON

Continue along the shore to the trattoria ❺ La Palanca

❸ Santa Maria della Presentazione

❹ Il Redentore

❺ La Palanca

(Mon–Sat noon–2.30pm, bar 7am–8.30pm | tel. 04 15 28 77 19 | €). Talk to owner Andrea and enjoy the excellent lunch or snacks and wonderful views of the Zattere from the waterside tables. If you want to have a quick look inland, *go down the Calle del Forno, then head left on Campo Junghans and follow Rio del Ponte Lungo until you reach the open water. About 700m further west,* you should definitely take a look at the ❻ Fortuny Showroom *(Mon–Fri 10am–1pm and 2–6pm | Fondamenta San Biagio 805)*, the showcase for Mariano Fortuny, the legendary Spanish designer and creator of luxury textiles – they are a feast for the eyes!

❻ Fortuny Showroom

The perfect way to end the day, *right nearby on the other side of the small canal,* is to go up to the roof of the Molino Stucky Hilton Hotel. Enjoy a pleasant drink in the ❼ Skyline Rooftop Bar *(daily noon–1am, Nov–March 4pm–1am)* as you admire the magical view of the city and its lagoon.

❼ Skyline Rooftop Bar

❹ THE LESSER-KNOWN LAGOON ISLANDS

➤ After a few days of city exploration, you'll be ready for island life
➤ Strolling, feasting and watching the world go by
➤ Nature and peace on Le Vignole, Sant'Erasmo and Lazzaretto Nuovo

📍 Fondamente Nove vaporetto stop

🏁 Lazzaretto Nuovo

→ approx. 10km

🚢 ½ day (total time on board approx. 1 hr; total walking time approx. 2 hrs

ⓘ Tours of ❻ **Lazzaretto Nuovo** only available at weekends between April and October

The best place to begin your tour is Venice's "vegetable island". It takes just 15 minutes by boat to get from the ❶ Fondamente Nove vaporetto stop to the island of

❶ Fondamente Nove

❷ Le Vignole

❸ Trattoria alle Vignole

❷ Le Vignole. *Walk along the main path from the jetty to the little bridge and cross over the main canal. Follow the right-hand path to* ❸ Trattoria alle Vignole *(closed Mon and Oct–March | tel. 04 15 28 97 07 | €).* The fish and meat dishes served on the simple wooden tables outside will taste particularly good alongside the silhouetted view of Venice! Only private boats with special authorization are permitted to access the famous maritime fortress of Sant'Andrea on the south- ern tip of the island. Constructed by the famous master builder Michele Sanmicheli in the 16th century, its canons once kept the enemies of the La Serenissima from approaching the city by sea.

MODERN ART ON SANT'ERASMO

❹ Sant'Erasmo

Further to the north, the island of ❹ Sant'Erasmo ➤ p.61 is a very peaceful place. It is Venice's second, but much larger "front garden". *Take a line 13 vaporetto from Le Vignole to get to the island's stop Capannone.*

❺ Torre Massimiliana

Walk about 15 minutes to the south to the ❺ Torre Massimiliana, a fortified brick tower that hosts inter- esting contemporary art exhibitions.

❻ Lazzaretto Nuovo

The little island of ❻ Lazzaretto Nuovo *lies across from the aforementioned Stazione Capannone.* Thanks to its strategic location, it has been used by the Venetians and different occupiers as a military base at different points in history. From the 15th to the 18th century, it

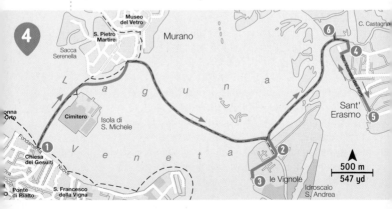

The patchwork of rural islands in the northern part of the lagoon

also protected La Serenissima against epidemics as it served as a quarantine station for people and goods. For some years now, archaeologists and ecologists have been devoting more attention to this long-neglected and almost forgotten island.

MULTIMEDIA TRIP TO THE PAST

As part of an "island revival" campaign, a team of local volunteers now offers highly recommended nature and history walks at weekends between April and October *(April–Oct Sat/Sun 9.45am and 4.30pm | tel. 04 12 44 40 11 | lazzarettonuovo.com)*. If you wish to take part in one of these tours, then *you need to board a vaporetto in Sant'Erasmo heading for Lazzaretto Nuovo around 4.15pm.* During the tour, which lasts about two hours, you will learn about Venice during the plague and you will get to see some of the defensive walls and huge warehouses – in particular the so-called Teson Grande filled with museum objects – as well as a documentary film. On the half-hour nature walk along the island's outer walls, information boards describe the flora and fauna found in the lagoon area.

GOOD TO KNOW

CITY BREAK BASICS

ARRIVAL

GETTING THERE

Venice is reached by car over the Ponte della Libertà causeway. We recommend that day visitors park in one of the – quite expensive and often full – multi-storey car parks near the historic centre around the Piazzale

RESPONSIBLE TRAVEL

Are you aware of your carbon footprint while travelling? You can offset your emissions (myclimate. org), plan your route with the environment in mind (routerank.com) and go gently on both nature and culture. For details of ecotourism in Italy and in general, please refer to ecotourism.org and findyour italy.com.

Roma or on Tronchetto Island. Both have recently been connected by a "people mover", an almost 900-m-long cable car on stilts (ticket: 1.50 euros). The car parks on the mainland in Fusina, Treporti and Punta Sabbioni are less expensive. A modern tram line connects Mestre and Venice via the Ponte della Libertà.

Venice can easily be reached by train from major cities all over Europe. But if you really want something different, try the Venice Simplon-Orient-Express (belmond.com). It is a privately run train of historic and beautifully restored coaches, providing a classic luxury train experience. It links London and Venice two or three times a month between April and November, the complete journey taking 24 hours and costing around 4,000 euros per person one way.

If you take a long-distance coach to Venice, you usually have to change

Take a *vaporetto* along the Canal Grande: public transport has never been such fun

coaches in Bolzano, Verona or Padua. The final stop for Flixbus is Mestre railway station, from where a local train gets you to Venice Santa Lucia or to the People Mover stop at Tronchetto in ten minutes.

A number of different major airlines such as British Airways *(british airways.com)* offer regular flights from the UK to Venice, from around £50 upwards, with prices averaging out at around £150 per person. Alitalia *(alitalia.com)* and several other international European airlines offer regular but not direct flights. Several no-frills airlines however do fly directly, e.g. easyJet *(easyjet.com)* and Ryanair *(ryanair.com)*, although not necessarily to Venice's main international airport. Some major carriers in the USA and Canada also offer direct flights as well as flights to major centres (Rome, London) and connecting flights to Venice.

Many cheaper flights are to Treviso airport located 20km inland *(treviso airport.it)*. From here a bus *(12 euros, return 22 euros | atvo.it)* takes you to the Piazzale Roma in Venice. Venice's international Marco Polo Airport is on the northern border of the lagoon in Tessera. There is also a bus from here *(8 euros, return 15 euros | atvo.it)* to the Piazzale Roma. As well as the very expensive water taxis, the *vaporetti* of the Alilaguna line *(alilaguna.it)* operate from Marco Polo airport to the islands of Murano *(8 euros)* and Lido *(15 euros)*, and in Venice itself to St Mark's Square *(15 euros)*. You can purchase tickets online at *venicelink. com* (slightly cheaper than in Venice itself). You may want to buy the combined *Venezia Unica City Pass (veneziaunica.it)*, which is a tourist pass that you can design and modify according to your needs.

CITY PASS VENEZIA UNICA

This personalized card is the cheapest way to take advantage of the public services in Venice. It is valid for seven days, making it easy for you to pick and choose your own agenda. Deals start with a basic offer, the San Marco City Pass for 38.90 euros. It includes free admission to the Doge's Palace, three other museums on St Mark's Square, three churches of your choice and the Museo Querini Stampalia. Various more expensive options include more museums, use of the *vaporetti*, airport transfers and the city's WiFi network. You can also add parking tickets and guided tours. The pass can be purchased online *(veneziaunica.it)* or at the *vaporetti* stops Tronchetto, Piazzale Roma, Rialto, Lido, Burano and Punta Sabbioni.

TOURIST TAX

What other cities have only imposed on motorists, now also applies to visitors in Venice: you have to pay a tourist tax called *contributo d'accesso* (access charge). The amount per person varies depending on the date and length of stay. On public holidays you pay more than on workdays, and during high season (April to October) more than during low season. If you arrive by train, you can pay this tax while still on board, otherwise on arrival or online at *veneziaunica.it*.

PORTERS

These helpers are sometimes extremely useful in this city of bridges and narrow streets, but they come at a price. They can be found at the railway station, Piazzale Roma, by the Accademia, near San Marco and the Hotel Danieli. Depending on distance, you could pay 50 euros or more to have your bags carried from the railway station or the Piazzale Roma to your hotel.

CLIMATE & WHEN TO GO

Venice has a moderate, Mediterranean climate. The hot sirocco wind blowing from Africa and the high humidity level can make it rather sticky in summer; the humidity is still there in winter when Venice can be cold and damp and, sometimes, foggy. From a climatic point of view, the best times to visit La Serenissima are April/May and September/October but some weeks in winter, when the air is crystal clear, have a very special charm. Look up the weather at *tempoitalia.it*.

GETTING AROUND

GONDOLAS

There are gondola ferries, so-called *traghetti*, that carry passengers across the Canal Grande for 2 euros per crossing at San Marcuola, near Santa Sofia next to the Ca' d'Oro, at the Riva del Carbon next to Rialto Bridge, near San Tomà, between San Samuele and Ca' Rezzonico, as well as by Santa Maria del Giglio.

PUBLIC TRANSPORT

By far the most practical form of transportation, and at the same time the one with the most flair, are the scheduled *vaporetti*, or water buses, operated by the municipal transport companies ACTV *(actv.it)*, although they are often overcrowded. They operate around two dozes lines on the Canal Grande and the main secondary canals, and also connect the city centre to the Lido, the lagoon islands and the mainland. However, a single ride costs an impressive 7.50 euros. So it's cheaper to buy a 24-hour ticket that will cost 20 euros, a two- or three-day ticket 30 and 40 euros respectively, and a week's ticket costs 60 euros.

Depending on the line, regular service starts in the morning between 5 and 7am, and ends between 8pm and 1am at night. Important for night owls: boats on the Canal Grande, the Giudecca Canal and to the Lido and northern lagoon islands also run all through the night on the *linee notturni*. Visit *actv.it* for everything about public transport routes, schedules and tariffs. Ticket desks and machines for *vaporetti* and buses are also to be found all over the city and on the islands. You will find a map with the precise locations at *trip planner.veneziaunica.it*.

TAXIS

The water taxis, so-called *motoscafi (tel. 04 15 22 23 03, 6pm–9am and Sat/ Sun 04 12 40 67 12 | motoscafivenezia. it)*, are a rather expensive option and are most suitable for small groups (up to a maximum of 10 people). Additional charges are made for more than two passengers, trips at night, telephone bookings, large pieces of luggage, etc. The most important stops are at the Piazzale Roma, the railway station, near Rialto Bridge, in San Marco, at the Lido and the airport.

Look out for the yellow signs to help you navigate your way through the city

EMERGENCIES

EMBASSIES & CONSULATES

BRITISH CONSULATE GENERAL
Via s. Paolo 7 | 20121 Milan | tel. (39) 02 72 30 01 | www.gov.uk/world/italy

U.S. CONSULAR AGENCY
at Venice Marco Polo Airport | General Aviation Terminal | Viale Galileo Galilei 30 – 30173 Tessera (VE) | tel. (39) 04 15 41 59 44 | https://it.usembassy.gov/embassy-consulates/milan/consular-agency-venice/

EMERGENCY SERVICES
Emergency: *tel. 112* | police: *tel. 113* | fire brigade: *tel. 115* | ambulance *tel. 118*

HEALTH
The European Health Insurance Card (EHIC), valid in Italy, is being phased out and is being replaced by the Global Health Insurance Card (GHIC). It is recommended that you take out travel healthcare insurance to cover the costs of private treatment. Your hotel will help you find an English-speaking doctor. In emergencies, the Santi Giovanni e Paolo Hospital can be reached at *tel. 04 15 29 41 11*, and the health centre on the Lido at *tel. 04 12 38 56 68*. The *pronto soccorso* section is responsible for emergency admission. Information on chemists open outside regular hours is posted or available from the telephone information service at *tel. 192*.

ESSENTIALS

ACCOMMODATION
There are plenty of hotels in Venice – in all parts of the city and for all budgets. It is recommended that you compare rates before booking. Value for money is often hard to find in Venice, and is highly dependent on the season.

A nice double room in a central location during high season – i.e. from Easter to the end of October, at Christmas, New Year and the Carnival – can easily set you back by 200 euros. It's cheaper if you visit in winter, when there are far fewer tourists in the city and the hotels offer reductions of 30 to 50 per cent. Another tip to save you some cash: the further away you are from St Mark's Square, the more reasonable the prices. The city now charges a tourist tax per person per night – the so-called *imposta di soggiorno* – of between 1 and 5 euros depending on the hotel category, and less during low season (by which they mean January only!).

In principle, you should always book in advance. Apart from the known hotel portals, the website *venicehotel.com* has a good selection of accommodation. We recommend that you check the hotel's website as well as the large international websites for special offers. When telephoning a hotel or when on site, always ask for a *sconto* (i.e. a discount), especially if you intend to stay for several nights. For families and groups, a holiday home might be a good option: you can rent them not just for an entire week, but also on a daily basis, and they will provide you with the facilities to prepare your own food.

BANKS & MONEY

There are cash dispensers throughout the city and major credit cards are accepted almost everywhere. In Venice, people tend to pay for smaller purchases in cash.

CUSTOMS

EU citizens can import and export for their personal use tax-free (e.g. 800 cigarettes, 1kg tobacco, 10 litres of spirits over 22%). Non-EU citizens can import and export for their personal use tax-free: 200 cigarettes, 250g tobacco, 4 litres of wine, 1 litre of spirits over 22%, 16 litres of beer. *visahq.com/italy/customs*.

GONDOLA RIDES

For many people, a romantic ⚑ ride in a gondola is one of the highlights of a visit to Venice. A half-hour ride in a gondola in a group of four to six people will usually cost around 80–160 euros. Individuals can obtain a seat in a gondola with other passengers by booking online, e.g. at *localvenicetours.com (28.80 euros/pers.)*. The gondolieri wait for their passengers at the Piazzetta San Marco, in front of the Hotel Danieli, behind St Mark's Square in the Bacino Orseolo, as well as along the Canal Grande at the Piazzale Roma, near the railway station at Campo Santa Sofia, by Rialto Bridge and the San Tomà, Giglio and Vallaresso *vaporetto* stops. Ask your gondoliere to turn off into the small side canals that are inaccessible to motor boats as soon as possible. This way you cruise silently on the water as they did in the good old days, unless your gondoliere treats you to an aria!

INSIDER TIP
Silently cruise the side canals

GUIDED TOURS

You can book officially authorised, English-speaking guides from the *Cooperativa Guide Turistiche (tel. 04 15 20 90 38 | guidevenezia.it)*. Individual guided tours start from approx. 100 euros (including admission to the Doge's Palace and St Mark's Basilica).

HOW MUCH DOES IT COST?

Vaporetto	7.50 euros for a single ticket
Gondola	80–160 euros for a 30-minute trip depending on the time of day
Snack	from 3 euros for a panino at the bar
Admission	20 euros combined ticket for the Doge's Palace and the museums on St Mark's Square
Wine	2 euros for a glass of white wine
Espresso	1.20–1.50 euros for an espresso standing at the bar

HIGH WATER

Acqua alta is almost a part of everyday Venetian life in the winter. If there is the threat of flooding, warning sirens are sounded throughout the entire city. The nightmare usually lasts for a few hours. There are maps in some *vaporetto* stops showing where there are wooden bridges that make it possible to reach your destination without getting your feet wet – even when the city is under water. The water-level forecast can be found on the internet at *ilmeteo.it/portale/marea-venezia*.

INFORMATION

Tourist Contact Center (daily 9am–2pm | tel. 04 15 29 87 11). Local information centres are at the railway station *(daily 7am–9pm)*, in the centre at the Museum Correr *(daily 9am–7pm)*, at the Piazzale Roma *(daily 7.30am–7.30pm)* and at Marco Polo airport *(daily 8.30am–7pm)*. Tourist information, ticket reservations and purchases for all sorts of events are also available at *veneziaunica.it* or in English or Italian at *tel. 0 41 24 24 (daily 7.30am–7pm)*.

The official website of the tourism association is *turismovenezia.it,* while *comune.venezia.it* – the digital presence of the city council – offers useful links. The city's museums have a joint and comprehensive website: *visitmuve.it*. You will find information about art, sports and other events in Italian and English at *unospitedivenezia.it* and *meetingvenice.it*. All kinds of information is also available at *introducing venice.com*, *venicewelcome.com* and *veneziatoday.it*, which features an events schedule in Italian.

Complaints about unsatisfactory public services or improper treatment of tourists can be submitted by email to *complaint.apt@turismovenezia.it*. During its normal business hours, the tourism association APT also offers assistance at *tel. 04 15 29 87 26*.

NATIONAL HOLIDAYS

1 Jan	Capodanno (New Year)
6 Jan	Epifania (Epiphany)
March/April	Pasquetta (Easter Monday)
25 April	Liberazione
	(Day of Liberation from Fascism)
1 May	Festa del Lavoro (Labour Day)
2 June	Giorno della Repubblica
	(Day of the Republic)
15 Aug	Ferragosto (Ascension Day)
1 Nov	Ognissanti (All Saints)
8 Dec	Immacolata Concezione
	(Immaculate Conception)
25 Dec	Natale (Christmas Day)
26 Dec	Santo Stefano (Boxing Day)

POSTAGE

Stamps *(francobolli)* can be bought in post offices or tobacconist's shops. Postage for postcards and standard letters to EU countries and the UK is 1.15 euros. Please note that there are several private competitors of the postal service, all with their own stamps. The disadvantage is that you have to drop your letters in those companies' designated letter boxes, which are few and far between. Make sure you ask explicitly for post office stamps!

INSIDER TIP
Buy the right stamps

TELEPHONE & WIFI

To phone the UK from Venice, use the country code 0044, for calls to the US 001. The country code for Italy is 0039, followed by the full telephone number including the '0' of the area code.

It possible for you to log in to the WiFi network and access the internet near St Mark's Square, free of charge. The only condition is that you purchase a museum ticket or pass online at *veneziaunica.it*. Most hotels now offer either a computer with internet for guest use or provide WiFi access (password protected) for smartphones, tablets or laptops.

TIPPING

A service charge is normally included, but waiters, hotel maids, gondoliers, etc. are naturally pleased if you reward them for their friendly service. Five to ten per cent is usual in restaurants: first, the waiter will give you your change in full, then you leave your tip on the table.

WHAT'S ON

The best way to find out about events, etc. is through the daily newspapers *Il Gazzettino* and *La Nuova Venezia* as well as the (Italian/English) pamphlets *Venezia News*, *Un Ospite di Venezia*, *Venezia da Vivere* and *Meeting Venice*. The last two are available free of charge at all arrival points, in many hotel receptions, at travel offices, etc.

WEATHER IN VENICE

High season
Low season

	JAN	FEB	MARCH	APRIL	MAY	JUNE	JULY	AUG	SEPT	OCT	NOV	DEC
Daytime temperature	6°	8°	12°	17°	21°	25°	28°	28°	24°	18°	12°	7°
Night-time temperature	1°	2°	5°	10°	14°	17°	20°	19°	17°	12°	7°	3°
Hours of sunshine per day	3	4	4	6	7	9	10	9	7	5	3	2
Rainy days per month	6	6	7	8	9	7	6	5	6	8	9	7
Sea temperature in °C	9	8	10	13	17	21	23	24	21	18	14	11

☀ Hours of sunshine per day ☂ Rainy days per month ≈ Sea temperature in °C

WORDS & PHRASES
IN ITALIAN

In Italian, an accent is only used if the last syllable is stressed, otherwise we have indicated the stressed syllable by placing a dot below the stressed vowel.

Yes/No/Maybe	sì/no/forse
Please/Thank you	per favore/grazie
Excuse me, please!	Scusa!/Scusi!
Pardon?	Come dice?/Prego?
Good morning/afternoon Good evening/Good night	Buon giorno!/Buon giorno!/Buona sera!/Buona notte!
Hello/ Goodbye/See you	Ciao!/Ciao!/Arrivederci!
My name is …	Mi chiamo …
What's your name?	Come si chiama?/Come ti chiami?
I would like to …/Have you got …?	Vorrei …/Avete …?
I (don't) like that	(Non) mi piace.
good/bad	buono/cattivo
ambulance/police/fire brigade	ambulanza/polizia/vigili del fuoco

SYMBOLS

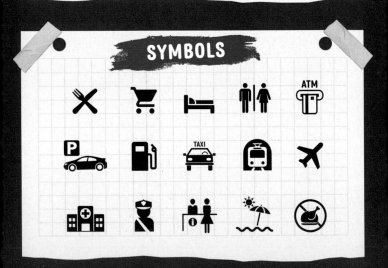

EATING & DRINKING

The menu, please	Il menù, per favore.
bottle/carafe/glass	bottiglia/caraffa/bicchiere
knife/fork/spoon	coltello/forchetta/cucchiaio
salt/pepper/sugar	sale/pepe/zucchero
vinegar/oil/milk/cream/lemon	aceto/olio/latte/panna/limone
with/without ice/sparkling	con/senza ghiaccio/gas
cold/too salty/not cooked	freddo/troppo salato/non cotto
vegetarian/allergy	vegetariano/vegetariana/allergia
May I have the bill, please?	Vorrei pagare, per favore.
bill/receipt/tip	conto/ricevuta/mancia
cash/credit card	in contanti/carta di credito

MISCELLANEOUS

Where can I find...?	Dove posso trovare ...?
left/right/straight ahead/back	sinistra/destra/dritto
What time is it?	Che ora è? Che ore sono?
It's three o'clock/It's half past three	Sono le tre./Sono le tre e mezza.
today/tomorrow/yesterday	oggi/domani/ieri
How much is ...?	Quanto costa ...?
too much/much/little/all/nothing	troppo/molto/poco/tutto/niente
expensive/cheap/price	caro/economico/prezzo
Where can I find internet access?	Dove trovo un accesso internet/wi-fi?
open/closed	aperto/chiuso
broken/doesn't work	guasto/non funziona
breakdown/repair shop	guasto/officina
schedule/ticket	orario/biglietto
train/track/platform	treno/binario/banchina
Help!/Attention!/Caution!	Aiuto!/Attenzione!/Prudenza!
prohibited/forbidden/danger/dangerous	divieto/vietato/pericolo/pericoloso
pharmacy	farmacia
fever/pain	febbre/dolori
0/1/2/3/4/5/6/7/8/9/10/100/1000	zero/uno/due/tre/quattro/cinque/sei/sette/otto/nove/dieci/cento/mille

HOLIDAY VIBES

FOR RELAXATION & CHILLING

FOR BOOKWORMS & FILM BUFFS

📖 COMMISSARIO BRUNETTI

An essential companion for visitors to Venice: the Venetian-by-choice Donna Leon has written more than two dozen crime stories featuring the police commissioner – so far.

📖 DEATH IN VENICE

Unadulterated melancholy characterises Thomas Mann's legendary novella (1911) which tells of an old man's love for a beautiful youth. Luchino Visconti's film (1971) is an all-time classic.

📖 THOSE WHO WALK AWAY

Patricia Highsmith's psychological thriller (1967) also takes place in the floating city.

🎥 DON GIOVANNI

Venice plays a picturesque main role in Joseph Losey's adaptation of Mozart's opera as well as in Federico Fellini's film *Casanova* (1976).

🎥 DON'T LOOK NOW

Crime writers are especially inspired by the unique, melancholic atmosphere: Daphne du Maurier set her short story in Venice. It was sensitively filmed by Nicholas Roeg in 1973.

PLAYLIST

0:58

▶ **ANDREA BOCELLI** – CON TE PARTIRÒ
Yearning, the sea and intense emotions.

▶ **PITURA FRESKA** – PAPA NERO
Joyful reggae from a Venice cult band who mainly sing in Venetian dialect.

▶ **RONDÒ VENEZIANO** – LA SERENISSIMA
A must-have at any masked ball! Grand orchestral music, modern, but in the style of Venetian Baroque.

▶ **VIRTUOSI DI VENEZIA** – LE QUATTRO STAGIONI
Vivaldi's classics performed by this Venetian chamber orchestra.

Your holiday soundtrack can be found on **Spotify** under MARCO POLO Italy

Or scan this code with the Spotify app

ONLINE

SHORT.TRAVEL/VEN3
The official video of the Flight of the Angel that opens the Carnival.

SHORT.TRAVEL/VEN4
An amateur cameraman shows how grotesque the vast cruise liners look in the lagoon.

SHORT.TRAVEL/VEN23
In five minutes, 13 beautiful spots on and around Venice's canals are captured – in slow motion and accompanied by the "Chorus of the Hebrew Slaves" from Verdi's *Nabucco*.

VENICEWIKI.ORG
Even if you don't speak Italian, this Wiki will provide you with valuable and useful information, ranging from Venetian songs to a dialect dictionary.

VENEZIAUNICA.IT/EN
The official tourist and travel information of Venice gives a good overview.

VENETIANCAT.BLOGSPOT.COM
This popular blog by writer Cat Bauer who has lived on the Canal Grande in Venice for a number of years is an insider's view of the expat life in Venice.

TRAVEL PURSUIT

THE MARCO POLO HOLIDAY QUIZ

Do you know what makes Venice tick? Test your knowledge of the idiosyncrasies and eccentricities of the city and its people. You will find the answers at the foot of the page, with more detailed explanations on pages 20 to 25.

❶ How much does a newly built gondola cost?
a) 10,000 euros
b) 15,000 euros
c) 20,000 euros

❷ The Carnival was forbidden by Napoleon. When did the Venetians start celebrating it again?
a) In 1843
b) In 1899
c) In 1979

❸ In which way is the Venetian dialect similar to Spanish?
a) The pronunciation of certain consonants
b) Many words end with an "s"
c) The "j" is pronounced like a "ch"

❹ With which item is St Mark's lion, Venice's heraldic animal, always depicted?
a) A book
b) A sword
c) A crown

❺ What was the role of the Council of Ten?
a) It opened the Carnival season
b) It monitored the doges
c) It decided on building applications for plots along the Canal Grande

❻ Which globetrotter was born in Venice?
a) Marco Polo
b) Amerigo Vespucci
c) Francisco Pizarro

Entrance to a palazzo from the Canal Grande

INDEX

WE WANT TO HEAR FROM YOU!

Did you have a great holiday? Is there something on your mind? Whatever it is, let us know! Whether you want to praise the guide, alert us to errors or give us a personal tip – MARCO POLO would be pleased to hear from you. Please contact us by email:

sales@heartwoodpublishing.co.uk

We do everything we can to provide the very latest information for your trip. Nevertheless, despite all of our authors' thorough research, errors can creep in. MARCO POLO does not accept any liability for this.

PICTURE CREDITS
Cover photo: Canal Grande (Schapowalow: M. Rellini)
Photos: DuMont Bildarchiv: S. Lubenow (86/87, 123); Getty Images: S. Blanco (116), M. Bottigelli (96/97), M. A. Paulda (12/13), M. Secchi (70); K. Hausen (135); huber-images: G. Baviera (11, 47, 95), W. Bertsch (50/51), M. Carassale (67, 84), F. Cogoli (22), L. Da Ros (35, 55), O. Fantuz (102/103), G. Gräfenhain (46, 104/105), S. Kremer (17, 40, 42, 81, 83, 100/101), F. Lukasseck (4, 6/7, 132), A. Piai (74, 91), M. Rellini (26/27, 36), G. Simeone (2/3); Laif: P. Adenis (52), N. Hilger (48), C. Kerber (109), H. Kloever (76/77); Laif/hemis.fr: A. Chicurel (32); Laif/Le Figaro Magazine: Martin (9, 73); Laif/Palladium: Burg + Schuh (31); Laif/robertharding: N. Clark (120/121); Look: K. Jäger (8, 112), K. Johaentges (14/15, 119), S. Lubenow (59); mauritius images: J. Warburton-Lee (62/63); mauritius images/age fotostock (124); mauritius images/Alamy: M. Scholz (92), Travelscapes (inside and outside cover flaps); mauritius images/Cultura: A. Weinbrecht (10); mauritius images/Westend61 (130/131); picture-alliance/NurPhoto: G. Cosua (25); Schapowalow/SIME: M. Carassale (21), L. Da Ros (38/39); vario image/MITO images: R. Niedring (98/99); vario images/Juice Images: I. Lishman (56); Shutterstock.com: Philippe Gregori (133)

4th Edition – fully revised and updated 2023
Worldwide Distribution: Heartwood Publishing Ltd, Bath, United Kingdom
www.heartwoodpublishing.co.uk

Authors: Kirstin Hausen, Walter M. Weiss
Editor: Nikolai Michaelis
Picture editor: Anja Schlatterer
Cartography: © MAIRDUMONT, Ostfildern (pp. 106–107, 110, 113, 115, 118, outside jacket, pull-out map; © MAIRDUMONT, Ostfildern, using data from OpenStreetMap, licence CC-BY-SA 2.0 (pp.28–29, 37, 45, 49, 53, 57, 60, 64–65, 78–79, 88–89)
Cover design and pull-out map cover design: bilekjaeger_Kreativagentur with Zukunftswerkstatt, Stuttgart
Page design: Langenstein Communication GmbH, Ludwigsburg

Heartwood Publishing credits:
Translated from the German by Thomas Moser, Robert McInnes, Jennifer Walcoff Neuheiser and Mo Croasdale
Editors: Felicity Laughton, Kate Michell, Sophie Blacksell Jones
Prepress: Summerlane Books, Bath
Printed in India

MARCO POLO AUTHOR
KIRSTIN HAUSEN

Venice is full of contrasts: this is what Kirstin noted at a press briefing on the Canal Grande at which photographer Oliviero Toscani presented his latest images: dead rats and rubbish floating in the canal. That was in 1999, and journalist Kirstin has been observing Venice's battle against its own demise ever since, all the while enjoying the fabulous aspects of the city.

DOS & DON'TS

HOW TO AVOID SLIP-UPS & BLUNDERS

DO KEEP YOUR SHIRT ON

No matter how hot it is, bare male or over-exposed female torsos or beachwear are taboo on the streets of the *centro storico*. And going into a church in that kind of get-up is not an option; you won't be let in.

DON'T ORDER PASTA AS A MAIN COURSE

It might be all right to fill up on a plate of pasta in a cheaper restaurant, but in classier restaurants there is an unwritten law that forbids this. Here, as elsewhere in Italy, pasta is a *primo piatto* and is followed by a main course of meat or fish. If you only need a snack, a *panino* or a couple of *tramezzini* at the bar would be a better idea.

DON'T EAT ON THE PIAZZA

An ever-increasing number of tourists have started taking a break on and near St Mark's Square and this has caused the authorities to ban sitting, drinking and eating on the Piazza, its steps, in the arcades, or on the Piazzetta by the jetties. The Giardini ex Reali, 150m away, has officially been declared the place where you can tuck into your food.

DON'T DODGE FARES

You might well be tempted, but be careful! Inspections are sometimes made on board *vaporetti* and, if you get caught without a ticket, it costs at least 50 euros.

DON'T DRAG YOUR SUITCASE OVER THE BRIDGES

Please carry your suitcase over the many little bridges in Venice. Dragging it over the steps will indeed cause the bridges to crumble – imagine how many millions of bag wheels bang against the steps every year. To say nothing of the noise they make…